BASICS

ILLUSTRATION

04

global
contexts

Ethical:
aware-
ness/
reflect-
ion/
debate

a
va
academia

An AVA Book
Published by AVA Publishing SA
Rue des Fontenailles 16
Case Postale
1000 Lausanne 6
Switzerland
Tel: +41 786 005 109
Email: enquiries@avabooks.ch

Distributed by Thames & Hudson (ex-North America)
181a High Holborn
London WC1V 7QX
United Kingdom
Tel: +44 20 7845 5000
Fax: +44 20 7845 5055
Email: sales@thameshudson.co.uk
www.thamesandhudson.com

Distributed in the USA & Canada by:
Ingram Publisher Services Inc.
1 Ingram Blvd.
La Vergne TN 37086, USA
Tel: +1 866 400 5351
Fax: +1 800 838 1149
Email: customer.service@ingrampublisherservices.com

English Language Support Office
AVA Publishing (UK) Ltd.
Tel: +44 1903 204 455
Email: enquiries@avabooks.ch

Copyright © AVA Publishing SA 2009

ISBN 978-2-940373-94-9

10 9 8 7 6 5 4 3 2 1

Design by Darren Lever

Cover image ('Airport') by Natsko Seki

Production and separations by:
AVA Book Production Pte. Ltd., Singapore
Tel: +65 6334 8173
Fax: +65 6259 9830
Email: production@avabooks.com.sg

All reasonable attempts have been made to trace,
clear and credit the copyright holders of the images
reproduced in this book. If any credits have been
inadvertently omitted, the publisher will endeavour
to incorporate amendments in future editions.

Ghosts
by Gary Embury

This illustration by Gary Embury was
inspired by 'Ghosts'; a novel by Paul Auster.

Table of contents

Introduction   6

How to get the most out of this book   10

Chapter One: The international dimension   12

Illustration and education   14

Illustration and professional practice   28

Projects   32

Chapter Three: Imaginary worlds   58

Folklore   60

Science fiction   66

Virtual worlds   72

Unexpected images   76

Projects   84

Chapter Five: Head, heart and hand   116

Head   118

Heart   122

Hand   128

Global responsibilities   132

Projects   136

Chapter Two: Social commentary and history   34

Art and industry   36

The satirical cartoon   42

Visual codes   52

Projects   56

Chapter Four: A universal language   86

Diagrams   88

East/West dialogues   94

Cultural roadmaps   100

Make 'em laugh   108

Projects   114

Chapter Six: A global community   138

World markets   140

Worldwide collaborations   144

Collectives   152

Projects   158

Appendix   160

Glossary   162

Global network charts   164

Reference material   168

Contacts   172

Conclusion   174

Acknowledgements   175

Working with ethics   177

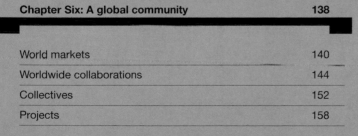

Introduction

Illustration is dead, long live illustration.

In the twenty-first century the field of illustration continues to evolve. The digital revolution has led to a convergence of technologies and media channels and an increased blurring of communication boundaries. Some claim that the word illustration, with its historical associations as a specialist activity, no longer reflects the explosion of exciting multifaceted, digital creativity now taking place. I have never had much time for this debate about categorising and labelling creative practice. However, if illustration is a rewarding, imaginative and applied art form and profession (the creating of purposed images for specific contexts, clients and audiences) then the term is still broad enough to align with the spirit of today's global activity.

The increasing visibility of illustration from advertising to graphic novels and animation to retail has led to fashionable hype declaring that illustration is the new graphic design (heralding the typographic comeback, no doubt) and the contemporary art world is also embracing illustrative storytelling.

This book does not concern itself with the old fine art vs commercial art debate; instead *Global Contexts* provides historical references from around the globe in order to contextualise the ideas and artwork presented.

All over the world, versatile, forward-thinking illustrators are having fun making pictures for defined contexts intended for reproduction while making a living by challenging convention and embracing open approaches and new strategies to the subject. Utilising the Internet, they are 'going global', exploring the discipline's history and its present and future possibilities, seeking clients, emerging markets, inspiration and imagery, sharing ideas, joining virtual communities, forming collectives, sending artwork and setting up online blogs, websites, portfolios, galleries and shops. Offline, in the real world, they are sharing studios, combining traditional skills with new technology, operating as multidisciplinary collectives, working with clients, printing posters, self-publishing, initiating gallery shows, travelling on world tours, creating street art and live painting performances.

This volume aims to take the reader on a journey through the international contemporary illustration landscape. It has been designed for dedicated art and design students, aspiring illustrators, professional image-makers and anyone interested in this vibrant and dynamic form of expression.

Greed by Eduardo Recife

Brazilian artist, illustrator and designer Eduardo Recife's work has a nostalgic quality and his doodles, 'stains' and textures merge with pencil-drawn and digital marks. 'Greed' (2007) is a personal project that incorporates digital collage, pencil and paint.

Global Contexts features intelligent, allusive, compelling, incisive, humorous and inspiring illustrations by leading exponents of the past, up-and-coming talent and outstanding international practitioners of this ever-changing and expanding discipline. The book also contains a series of progressive and practical illustration assignments addressing commercial and social aims, global issues and concerns including climate change, sustainable development and globalisation, which are deployed throughout the book to echo and extend the themes discussed. The text is also supplemented with valuable advice and details on the capabilities of materials, tools, techniques and equipment, creative working processes and methodologies, influential movements, major current trends and debates, emerging global markets, promotional strategies, freelancing, making a living, ethical implications and professional business practices.

Through a broad and contextual approach to this fascinating branch of the arts this volume illuminates the rich historical development of illustration, its influential contribution to civilisations of the past and continuing cultural significance, and its promising future.

Chapter One: The international dimension

This chapter considers illustration as a socially, historically, culturally and globally significant art form and explores the issues facing illustration students and practitioners.

Chapter Two: Social commentary and history

Introduces the illustrator as the inventor of imaginary worlds through examples of book and magazine illustration, which have interpreted folklore, legends, myths, fantasy and science fiction.

Chapter Three: Imaginary worlds

Addresses themes and explores the importance of illustrators engaging with their own content and subject matter and presents contemporary examples of graphic commentary and agitation related to global issues and concerns.

Chapter Four: A universal language

Highlights the role of the Internet in the establishment of illustration as a global activity and an international community without borders.

Chapter Five: Head, heart and hand

The influential and ongoing cross-pollination of visual languages between the East and the West is explored in detail. An overview of the role of humour in illustration is also introduced with both historical and contemporary examples of works of wit and satire.

Chapter Six: A global community

Explores the professional and collaborative activity of illustration and the solving of visual communication problems in a broad range of contexts worldwide. This chapter also provides entrepreneurial strategies and advice for working as a freelance illustrator.

Sophie
by Izzie Klingels

This image was used as a promotional
flyer for an exhibition of 'Klingels' work
and was inspired by a photo of her teenage
niece draped in the American flag.

How to get the most out of this book

This book introduces different aspects of illustration in global contexts via dedicated chapters for each topic. Each chapter provides numerous examples of work by leading artists, with interview quotes to explain their rationales, methodologies and working processes. Key illustration principles are isolated so that the reader can see how they are applied in practice.

Additional information
Captions are featured where necessary, as is client, illustrator and image information.

Written explanations
Key points are explained and placed in context.

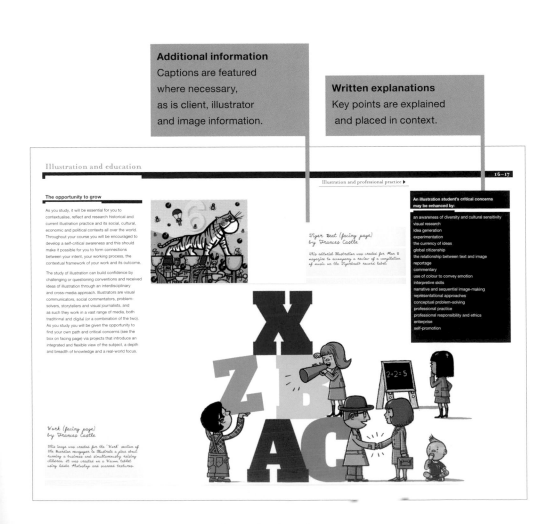

Illustration and professional practice ▶

The opportunity to grow

As you study, it will be essential for you to contextualise, reflect and research historical and current illustration practice and its social, cultural, economic and political contexts all over the world. Throughout your course you will be encouraged to develop a self-critical awareness and this should make it possible for you to form connections between your intent, your working process, the contextual framework of your work and its outcome.

The study of illustration can build confidence by challenging or questioning conventions and received ideas of illustration through an interdisciplinary and cross-media approach. Illustrators are visual communicators, social commentators, problem-solvers, storytellers and visual journalists, and as such they work in a vast range of media, both traditional and digital (or a combination of the two). As you study you will be given the opportunity to find your own path and critical concerns (see the box on facing page) via projects that introduce an integrated and flexible view of the subject, a depth and breadth of knowledge and a real-world focus.

Tiger Beat (facing page)
by Frances Castle

This editorial illustration was created for Men 2 magazine to accompany a review of a compilation of music on the Tigerbeat6 record label.

An illustration student's critical concerns may be enhanced by:

an awareness of diversity and cultural sensitivity
visual research
idea generation
experimentation
the currency of ideas
global citizenship
the relationship between text and image
reportage
commentary
use of colour to convey emotion
interpretive skills
narrative and sequential image-making
representational approaches
conceptual problem-solving
professional practice
professional responsibility and ethics
enterprise
self-promotion

Work (facing page)
by Frances Castle

This image was created for the 'Work' section of the Guardian newspaper to illustrate a piece about running a business and simultaneously raising children. It was created on a Wacom tablet using Adobe Photoshop and scanned textures.

Introductions
Special section introductions outline basic concepts that will be discussed.

Clear navigation
Each chapter has a clear running head to allow readers to quickly locate areas of interest.

Examples
Commercial projects from contemporary illustrators bring the principles under discussion visually alive.

Quotes
Quotes from featured illustrators and from artists throughout history are included.

Projects
The assignments are designed to build confidence, extend skills and encourage you to solve visual communication problems by drawing on your own experience and imagination.

Illustration is the pictorial matter that clarifies and enhances text. Communication, narrative and storytelling are at the heart of illustration and illustrators do not simply explain an author's work; instead they collaborate with the author in order to *amplify* the text.

Illustration has long been used as a cultural tool of communication to inform, provoke, persuade and entertain. As such, it has made an important contribution to our interpretation and understanding of the world. Images have transmitted patterns of behaviour and advanced a range of intellectual and social processes, which in turn have led to the formation of groups of people around the world. There are now 6.7 billion people on the planet and this figure is predicted to grow to nine billion by 2042. The world needs illustration now more than ever to make sense of human interactions, tell stories and to pictorially interpret our lives.

This book considers illustration as a socially, historically, culturally and globally significant art form. Intersecting themes are explored to highlight the realities facing the student illustrator or emerging practitioner in today's global environment. These themes include the impact of the Internet; the effect of globalisation on illustration education and practice; how cross-cultural and transglobal relationships affect illustrators' work; and professional, ethical and environmental responsibilities.

This chapter will:

Introduce undergraduate education in illustration, intercultural perspectives and professional practice.

Explore key principles for constructing images and work in a broad variety of media and contexts.

Demonstrate the importance of strategic planning and playing to your strengths in order to succeed in freelance practice.

Explorer by Gemma Correll

This collage image was created for 'The Other Project' exhibition (2007) and explores the theme of what children want to do when they grow up.

The growth of the creative industries, and of an information-based society and a knowledge-based economy, are fuelling an increasing demand for new visual content. As well as a passion for the subject, today's illustrators need to develop skills that will enable them to manage change in a demanding global environment.

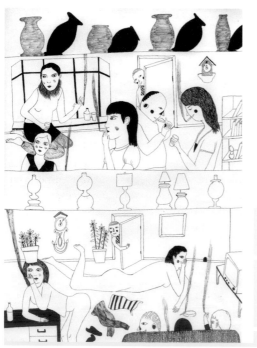

Part 2 (left) and Part 3 (above) by Mike Redmond

These two drawings are scenes taken from the same narrative project. Drawn with biro pen they work together through light and shadow.

Diverse approaches

Longevity in illustration is achieved by developing a creative, consistent and personal visual language, by reading and researching content, by technical accomplishment and from understanding the cultural and professional contexts. Many of today's illustration courses are written specifically to allow students to develop both discipline-specific skills and generic and transferable key skills (such as IT proficiency, effective communication, working with others and problem-solving). As a rule, students of illustration are given the opportunity to learn both these skill sets throughout their course and these provide a valuable foundation for professional practice.

The three main overlapping areas in illustration education are practical, critical-thinking and professional skills. In many cases, course content and delivery is informed by international and cross-cultural perspectives to prepare students with the skills needed to be able to work as illustrators anywhere in the world. Cultural intelligence and sensitivity is encouraged, as are collaborative learning activities that facilitate dialogue on professional practice in different countries.

All forms of visual communication are ideas-led; therefore the ability to generate, analyse and develop ideas is also at the core of illustration. Illustrators learn by creating, therefore visual literacy and the ability to record and develop ideas through drawing are essential. Life drawing is a regular course activity that is practised to build strong and confident drawing skills. Drawing from visual memory and from imagination often complements objective and analytical drawing, and the combination of these techniques will allow you to develop a personal visual language and the ability to generate, manipulate and articulate ideas in response to set briefs and deadlines. However, it's important to keep in mind that these techniques are a means to an end, not an end in themselves.

Illustration borrows many principles from the fields of design and fine art that provide guidelines for the construction of illustrated images.

These principles are concerned with:

- perceptual skills
- perspective and foreground
- middle ground and background
- space and depth
- relative dimensions
- positive and negative
- texture
- direction
- line
- shape
- form
- composition
- colour
- value
- unity and harmony
- balance
- focal point
- contrast
- proportion
- repetition
- pattern
- rhythm
- consistency
- movement
- the rule of thirds

The 'best practice' guidelines in each of these areas can be organised, followed or broken depending on the purpose of the image you are creating, and an understanding of the 'rules' in each one will provide you with a solid visual vocabulary.

Illustration and education

The opportunity to grow

As you study, it will be essential for you to contextualise, reflect and research historical and current illustration practice and its social, cultural, economic and political contexts all over the world. Throughout your course you will be encouraged to develop a self-critical awareness and this should make it possible for you to form connections between your intent, your working process, the contextual framework of your work and its outcome.

The study of illustration can build confidence by challenging or questioning conventions and received ideas of illustration through an interdisciplinary and cross-media approach. Illustrators are visual communicators, social commentators, problem-solvers, storytellers and visual journalists, and as such they work in a vast range of media, both traditional and digital (or a combination of the two). As you study you will be given the opportunity to find your own path and critical concerns (see the box on facing page) via projects that introduce an integrated and flexible view of the subject, a depth and breadth of knowledge and a real-world focus.

Work (facing page)
by Frances Castle

This image was created for the 'Work' section of The Guardian newspaper to illustrate a piece about running a business and simultaneously raising children. It was created on a Wacom tablet using Adobe Photoshop and scanned textures.

An illustration student's critical concerns
may be enhanced by:

an awareness of diversity and cultural sensitivity
visual research
idea generation
experimentation
the currency of ideas
global citizenship
the relationship between text and image
reportage
commentary
use of colour to convey emotion
interpretive skills
narrative and sequential image-making
representational approaches
conceptual problem-solving
professional practice
professional responsibility and ethics
enterprise
self-promotion

Tiger Beat (facing page)
by Frances Castle

This editorial illustration was created for *Plan B* magazine to accompany a review of a compilation of music on the *Tigerbeat6* record label.

An inter-cultural perspective

An international dimension is embedded in most art and design courses to encourage students to understand the global context of illustration. This understanding will help you to operate effectively in professional environments and engage on the international stage.

During the nineteenth century Industrial Revolution, Britain was known as the workshop of the world. In the twenty-first century countries such as China, Japan, the USA and India are spearheading a new industrial revolution. This revolution is focused on the interconnected global economy, new technologies and media and the exchange of information by globally connected computer networks. Human capital (the stock of skills and knowledge embodied in the ability to perform a function so as to produce economic value) is now seen as an important tool for generating economic benefits around the world.

Studio culture at college

Students working in the studios at Camberwell College of Arts in London on collaborative illustration project briefs. An international and intercultural perspective was embedded in the content of the illustration project briefs (which were either self-directed by students or set by the author). Camberwell has multicultural cohorts of students from over 100 countries around the world. Throughout the course, diverse perspectives are fostered and students draw on their personal experiences and different backgrounds.

Analogue and digital

Any undergraduate illustration course will provide a studio environment and access to workshops from the outset. This will expose you to a broad spectrum of media and creative low-fi analogue and digital techniques such as:

- life drawing and painting
- observational, location and off-site drawing
- idea generation
- lateral thinking
- concepts
- visual metaphors
- video editing
- animation
- web and imaging software
- the use of cameras, scanners and printers
- experimental mark-making
- mixed media
- printmaking
- photography
- 3-D illustrative sculpture
- bookbinding and construction
- 'zine and comic-book making
- moving image
- games development and design
- professional portfolio building
- experimental typography

Visual storytelling

Visual storytelling is at the heart of illustration; it involves the elucidation and amplification of texts provided (either by an author or written by the illustrator). The study of elements such as sequence, mood, atmosphere, characterisation and rhythm will enhance your visual editing skills and help you to develop a sympathy for the text.

Madonna in Ecstasy
by Mario Hugo

Mario Hugo creates emotive images by first joining pieces of paper torn from old books and then drawing on the sheet with china ink, graphite, gouache or acrylic. This image was created in 2008 for Dazed and Confused magazine.

Illustration and professional practice ▶

You will typically study illustration through project-based learning and will be encouraged to question the function of the project briefs that are set. Project briefs are often open-ended and oblique in order to encourage you to explore and create unpredictable experiences and engender innovative concepts, playfulness and perhaps a little chaos. For example, contemporary editorial illustration projects might introduce you to stand-alone images, idea generation, constraints, research, conceptual thinking and the application of visual metaphors, similes, analogies, comment and humour.

'No amount of skilful invention can replace the essential element of imagination'

Edward Hopper

And it was Left Void...
by Mario Hugo

This image is one of Mario's favourites and was created for his 'I've Got Something I'd Like to Show You' solo show at Vasava's Vallery. The image is drawn in graphite on found paper.

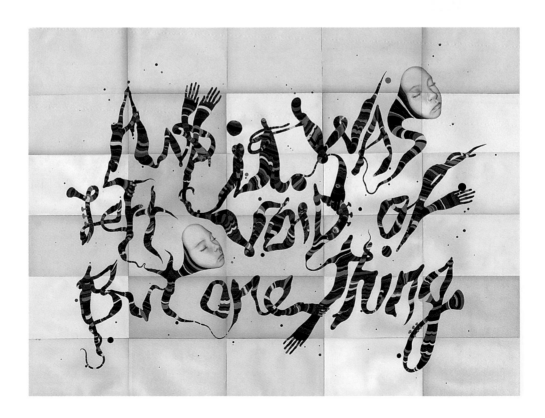

Matilda Tristram
by David Fulford

This striking pencil portrait was made for a catalogue of Royal College of Art animation graduates.

Untitled
by David Fulford

This dynamic portrait of the illustrator's mother was painted after an image distilled from a series of photographic sittings in which he used a wide-angle lens to capture an immediate and candid expression.

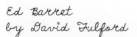

Ed Barret
by David Fulford

This graphite on paper portrait was created by former Camberwell College of Arts illustration student and RCA graduate David Fulford.

Surfing the waves of change

The study of illustration is a structured and supported process that will enable you to develop appropriate skills and knowledge for your own personal education and career development. Your course will prepare you to exploit the convergence of digital media in order to combine your unique personal visual language, image-making and storytelling skills with more generic skills and multidisciplinary methods.

Illustration is in a constant state of flux and there are now more opportunities than ever to surf the waves of change. In recent years, illustrators have had to deal with considerable threats such as clients purchasing generic stock illustrations rather than original work, attempts by clients to take ownership of copyrights and a decrease in traditional editorial work in printed media.

Contemporary illustrators have responded by establishing a new, dynamic and fluid global profession. They continue to cross-pollinate both design and fine art approaches with gallery exhibitions, self-published products, interiors, games, short films, animation and authored graphic narratives. Success in this highly competitive field depends on passion, creativity, originality, distinctiveness, flexibility and hard work: all areas that are prioritised during the study of illustration.

Plan B
by Gemma Correll

This quirky and humorous illustration for Plan B magazine combines Correll's offbeat wit with line drawing, collage and digital tools.

Field notes
by Gemma Correll

This spot illustration was created for Walrus magazine and was used as a header image for the magazine's 'Field notes' section (stories from around the world).

Primary Teachers
by Gemma Correll

This collage and digital image was created
to accompany an article in Primary Teachers
magazine, discussing a pilot scheme for
school tests.

Illustration and professional practice ▶

*Third Sector
by Frances Castle*

Castle created this simple, effective and dynamic image to accompany an article about being successful while working for a charity.

PPD

An important strand in current illustration education is personal and professional development (PPD), a process by which illustration students are encouraged to develop reflective and independent learning. Focus is placed on research and communication skills that will allow you to reflect on progress and achievement. PPD programmes also ask you to undertake strategic planning, and position yourself in the wider professional and commercial context of illustration.

Critically reflecting on strengths and weaknesses is a continuous process. It builds confidence and involves making and setting goals and objectives for developing skills, working independently and taking responsibility for your work. In addition, marketing for entry into the global market, project management, understanding the pricing of work, licensing, presentations to clients and creating a business and career plan are all part of being an illustrator and are core areas of study. This is good preparation for professional practice.

Illustration and professional practice

Illustration is where art meets business. To succeed in this highly demanding, rewarding and challenging global profession, you will have to face up to the realities of professional practice. Keep updating and identifying the overall priorities of mission, vision and values through comprehensive planning and strategic alignment; doing so will place a tighter focus on what matters.

'Whatever you believe you can do, begin it; boldness ha.

Directional beacons

Directional 'beacons' will help you to identify goals that detail where you want to be, objectives that list what you want to do and actions that outline how you are going to do it. Strategic analytical tools such as SWOT (Strengths, Weaknesses, Opportunities and Threats) charts or PEST (Political, Economic, Social and Technological) analysis can be utilised to find and establish the driving forces in your working environment and help you to achieve new objectives (for example, finding new markets, increasing efficiency or launching a new product).

enius, power and magic in it'

Goethe

A SMART approach

It's common for illustration students to work together on group projects in preparation for working in a complex global communications industry that operates through collaboration. Illustrators need a proactive approach to staying ahead of industry developments, navigating change, meeting deliverables and creating value for clients. It's often said that if you can measure it you can manage it, and using the SMART approach to writing action plans means that the objectives you set yourself should be Specific, Measurable, Attainable, Relevant and Timed. Against each objective, you should list a set of steps that can be used to work towards your strategic goals and specific results.

The SMART approach can be used to establish clear action plans to accomplish a changing set of objectives. Operational plans contain additional detail. These plans focus on the short-term objectives, specify the day-to-day and the year's major activities and projects, detail the allocation of operational budgets, specify different resource requirements, outline the division of responsibilities and timelines for each objective and critically specify who needs to do what and by when.

Both action and operational plans provide a framework for monitoring, updating, reviewing and evaluating measurable and specific goals.

CCTV
by Frazer Hudson

Characterised by strong concepts, Frazer Hudson's work is informed by a solid grounding in traditional drawing skills.

Play to your strengths

To be a self-employed freelance illustrator takes commitment and courage. It requires you to set goals, believe in yourself, follow your passion and do what you love, remembering that failure is not an option, not to give up, to be accountable for your actions and to learn from your mistakes. Successful illustrators in the business environment are those that keep developing their craft by pushing themselves every day, by being persistent and by finding the best way to make money out of something they love doing.

Self-awareness and brutal honesty is the first step towards succeeding in the marketplace. Take some time to discover what drives you, identify your strengths and weaknesses and ask yourself what you want to be doing in five or ten years' time. Be different and be better than the competition, tell your own story, identify what makes you special, then make sure the world knows about it.

Marketing activity can position your brand and create demand for your product. A strong marketing strategy that is updated and modified on a regular basis will allow you to attract and retain customers. Gather information on and enhance your Four P's (Product, Price, Place and Position – these are collectively known as the 'marketing mix') to effectively research your market, fix a pricing strategy and create advertising and promotional plans.

When determining your marketing strategy, conveying your unique selling proposition (USP) is key as it will define your competitive advantage and let clients know what makes your product special. The USP is used in marketing materials to attract and keep customers buying your products while defining what makes your products or services significantly different to the competition. In determining your USP, the key is to adopt a 'can-do' attitude by taking action quickly, seeing what others are doing (and more importantly what they are not doing) and then acting on the research.

'U R a Rock Star'
by Al Heighton

This image was hand drawn, scanned and then redrawn digitally with the use of a mouse. It was created as a self-promotional poster for the illustrator.

Projects ▶

Projects

Project 1:
Six cognitive levels

Create a series of six illustrated heads that interpret the six cognitive levels of behavioural complexity in Bloom's Taxonomy of Educational Objectives:

1 Knowledge: the recall of information
2 Comprehension: the translation, interpretation or extrapolation of knowledge
3 Application: the application of knowledge to a new situation
4 Analysis: the breaking down of knowledge into parts and the relationships between these parts
5 Synthesis: bringing together pieces of knowledge to form a whole and build relationships for new situations
6 Evaluation: judgments about the value of material and methods for given purposes

Research areas such as, conceptual illustration, visual metaphors, symbolism and both representational and abstract imagery.

Project 2:
Emerging markets

Create a series of illustrations for a magazine on the theme of emerging markets around the world offering new opportunities for designers, illustrators and architects. Research cities such as Dubai, Qatar, Abu Dhabi, Shanghai and Mumbai.

Project 3:
Colour

Design and illustrate a brochure for designers and illustrators to inform them of the importance of colour in producing work for different cultures. Research the cultural associations, emotional responses, traditions and psychological symbolism of colour throughout the world.

Project 4:

Sustainable development

Illustrate a series of posters to promote sustainable development that is meaningful to different cultures across the world. Research the issues surrounding sustainable development and study cultural and population differences.

Creating meaning is the most important issue in cross-cultural design and your artwork will have different emotional responses within different cultures. Your aim is to highlight issues and promote social interaction within the global community to effect change. The illustrations have to take into account respect for human diversity in order that this important message is clearly communicated and encourages the building of inclusive sustainable societies.

Project 5:

Jargon

Produce a double-page editorial illustration on the strange way business communicates to itself. Research and incorporate the following business jargon:

- Across the piece
- Alpha pup
- Arrows to fire
- Boiling the ocean
- Blue-sky thinking
- Win–win situation
- Parked offline
- Talk turkey
- Shoot the puppy
- Resource intensive

For inspiration, investigate the work of William Hogarth, Saul Steinberg, Peter Arno, Sue Coe, Ralph Steadman, Steve Bell and Kennard Phillipps.

Project 6:

Emotional response

Consider the following emotions:
Fear, anger, optimism, envy, remorse, awe, love, surprise, disgust, longing, malice, delight, sympathy, lust, pride, rapture, sadness, exasperation, anxiety, anticipation, compassion, acceptance, contempt, grief, timidity, hatred, greed, shame, respect, pity, courage, wonder, jealousy, despondency, horror, torment, modesty, revenge, happiness.

Act out the emotions in your imagination and consider how tensions and psychological effects can be created. Now produce an illustration for each of the emotions. Demonstrate the use of some of the following principles and elements in your designs: contrast, depth and perspective, direction, variety, dominating features, shape, proportion, scale, pattern, rhythm, repetition, harmony, balance, composition, texture, symmetry and asymmetry, positive and negative space, shade or colour, warm, cool and neutral colours.

An Excrescence;— a Fungus;—alias— a **Toadstool** upon a Dunghill.

Pub.ᵈ Dec.ʳ 20.ᵗʰ 1791. by H. Humphrey N.º 18. Old Bond Street.

The professional practice of illustration is an applied art form; illustrators often elucidate the ideas of others in order to communicate and appeal to a specific audience. As a student of illustration, you will be encouraged to find your own unique path by integrating the development of your practical skills with intellectual curiosity and theoretical analysis. Studying the history of art and illustration will also inform your practice and will allow you to engage in a constantly evolving area of debate.

Throughout history, illustration has long been employed as a powerful tool with which to comment on a wide range of social issues and influence the thinking of the day. Caricature (the distortion and exaggeration of a person's distinctive characteristics while preserving their likeness) has often been used as a weapon by illustrators to mock, offend or ridicule the powerful. The use of such satirical visual polemic has often led to controversy and outrage. For example, in the 1830s Charles Philipon's newspaper, *Le Charivari,* was heavily fined and the illustrator (Honoré Daumier) imprisioned for publishing an illustration that depicted King Louis-Philippe as a pear.

This chapter will explore how illustration has played an important role in fuelling, celebrating, condemning and chronicling revolution and struggles for freedom and justice; ranging from the English and American civil wars, to the world wars of the twentieth century and our own century's conflicts.

This chapter will:

Explore the historical, technical, ideological and cultural development of illustration and the way in which it reflects the conscience of humanity.

Introduce the visual codes used by illustrators. Review examples of historical and contemporary practice.

Provide practical illustration projects that enhance the understanding of the themes introduced.

William Pitt the Younger as a ' Toadstool upon a Dunghill'

This illustration by James Gillray, (1757-1815) of Pitt the Younger as a toadstool upon a dunghill uses graphic metaphor and irreverent humour to imply that Pitt's power stemmed from royal favours.

Art and industry

The technical advances of the Industrial Revolution in nineteenth-century Britain led to the mass production of printed matter for a growing urban population that was hungry for information. Thousands of illustrated books and periodicals were published and the period witnessed constant technical invention and experimentation including the power platen presses of the 1840s, wood, copper and steel engraving and the introduction of lithography, chromolithography, electrotyping, photolithography, photogravure, tonal printing, collotype and line blocks.

Wood engraving

During this period, wood engraving became a popular technique amongst illustrators. The image was incised on to the end grain of the wood with a burin, producing finer lines than woodcuts. Illustrations were cut by professional engravers on to the wooden blocks and printed rapidly on the new steam presses. This form of engraving became an affordable alternative to lithography and the most popular way of printing images for a growing market for all kinds of books and periodicals. Thomas Bewick had revolutionised the technique in the 1790s by producing meticulous vignettes and tailpieces depicting rural life for his *A General History of Quadrupeds* (1790) and *History of British Birds* (1797 and 1804).

Entertain and inform

The rise in urban populations and the expansion of the middle classes during this period led to a proliferation of periodicals and an increasing demand for pictorial information of all kinds. This launched the profession of illustration, making household names of graphic humourists, satirists and reporters such as John Leech, Frederic Villiers, Hubert von Herkomer, Honoré Daumier, Winslow Homer, Thomas Nast, René Bull and John Tenniel.

Periodicals such as *Le Charivari* (1832), *Punch* (1841), *The Illustrated London News* (1842), *L'illustration*, *Harper's Weekly* (1857), *Illustrated Newspaper* (1852), *Puck* (1871) and *The Graphic* (1869) flourished by providing pictorial records of events including adventures, disasters, murders, expeditions, inventions, state occasions and romantic interpretations of wars that entertained and informed their readership. Reporters known as special artists took their pencils, brushes, inks and sketchbooks to conflicts such as the Crimean War (1854–6) and the American Civil War (1861–5) in order to rapidly sketch battle scenes and post them back to their periodicals where in-house artists and engravers redrew the artwork on to a block for publication,

The satirical cartoon ▶

Capture of the Heights of Fredericksburg by Thomas Nast

Thomas Nast (1840–1902) was the father of American political cartooning and was influenced by Doré and Tenniel. His incisive pictorial journalism was committed to political and social justice.

CAPTURE OF THE HEIGHTS OF FREDERICKSBURG

'Here we make our bow, determined to pursue our great experiment with boldness, determined to keep continuously before the eye of the world a living and moving panorama of all its activities and influences'

From the *Illustrated London News* (1842)

À de Vresse, R Rivoli, 55-   Lith Destouches, R · Paradis · P.ᵗᵉ 88

L'Equilibre Européen.

Actualities –
The European Equilibrium
by Honoré Daumier

Known as the political pencil of Le Charivari,
Daumier produced hundreds of lithographs
that commented on social injustice and political
life in nineteenth-century France.

Meaningful illustration

A strand that resonates throughout the history of illustration is the creation of pictorial records of events in order to evoke compassion and prod the viewer's social conscience.
This tradition continues today in the work of editorial illustrators, gag-cartoonists, graphic novelists and political cartoonists, and in the work of contemporary reportage, documentary film-makers and photographers.

Key exemplars that captured the spirit of their time with great empathy include Théophile Alexandre Théophile Steinlen (1859–1923), who observed and chronicled the everyday lives of people in periodicals such as *Le Chat Noir*. Otto Dix (1891–1969) produced prints and paintings of the First World War and his work commented on the social turmoil of the Weimar Republic. Vladimir Mayakovsky (1894–1930), the outstanding poet and graphic artist of the Soviet Revolution, produced avant-garde posters and illustrations in support of the revolution's cause. Pablo Picasso (1881–1973), often described as the most important artist of the twentieth century, painted the groundbreaking *Guernica* in 1937 to express his revulsion at the bombings carried out during the Spanish Civil War.

This thought-provoking tradition also flows through the work of graphic satirists and commentators later in the twentieth and twenty-first centuries, as can be seen in the cases of Tomi Ungerer, Seymour Chwast, Milton Glaser, Saul Steinberg, Marshall Arisman, Brad Holland, Ronald Searle, Jules Feiffer, André François, Edward Sorel, David Levine, Fluck and Law, Ralph Steadman, Steve Bell, Sue Coe, Banksy and Peter Kennard.

Ratio 5
by Thomas Barwick

This menacing character appears in Tom Barwick's
twisted cinematic graphic novel/magazine 'Ratio'.

Inyenzi (above)
and Rwanda (right)
by Paul Bowman.

These pictures offer comment on the Balkans
war and the genocide in Rwanda in the 1990s.
Both conflicts led to people who had previously
grown up and lived together turning on each
other with horrific consequences.

The satirical cartoon ▶

The satirical cartoon

The tradition of satirical graphic commentary has a long and rich heritage, from fifteenth-century woodcut prints, pamphlets, broadsides and chapbooks to the eighteenth-century engravings of William Hogarth, Francisco Goya, James Gillray, Thomas Rowlandson and George Cruikshank.

Punch

The genre reached large audiences in nineteenth-century Britain with the publication of a number of satirical journals. One such example was the iconic weekly British magazine *Punch,* which was named after the puppet Mr Punch (or Punchinello). It was originally subtitled *the London Charivari* after the French illustrated satirical magazine and was published between 1841 and 1992 and again from 1996 to 2002.

In 1843, *Punch* was credited with the first use of the word 'cartoon' to describe humorous and satirical drawings. It provided exposure for some of the greatest chroniclers and critics of topical events of the day including Richard Doyle (also credited with designing *Punch's* masthead), John Leech, Phil May, Charles Keene, George Du Maurier, John Tenniel and EH Shepard.

Before 1843, illustrators producing witty, ironic and satirical images for reproduction were described as caricaturists; after 1843 they became cartoonists. John Leech is credited with changing the use of the term with his work for *Punch*. Outstanding exponents of *Punch* cartooning artwork included Max Beerbohm, John Hassall, Donald McGill, W Heath Robinson, David Low and HM Bateman.

Gladstone

William Ewart Gladstone
by Phil May

Illustrating with wit and economy of line, regular Punch and Graphic cartoonist Phil May showed real empathy for his subject matter. His swift use of pen and ink was influenced by the great Caran D'Ache.

Émile Coué (1857–1926) from the
cover of 'Simplicissimus' magazine,
12th December 1925 (colour litho)
By Thomas Theodor Heine

Heine was a co-founder of Simplicissimus
and created 2500 drawings for the magazine.
His work appeared on the front page more
than any other artist. He was regarded as
the greatest German draughtsman.

Simplicissimus

The influential German magazine *Simplicissimus* was far less whimsical than *Punch*. Founded in 1896 by publisher Albert Langen and artist Thomas Theodor Heine, *Simplicissimus* combined biting satirical and political commentary with striking graphic art including work by Heine, Olaf Gulbransson, Karl Arnold, Edward Thony and George Grosz. Attacks in the magazine on society, government, clergy and the Prussian military led to prison sentences for Heine and greatly increased the magazine's popularity.

Inspired by *Simplicissimus*, New York magazine *The Masses* (1911–1918) combined art and socialist political views and featured striking illustrations of everyday life by realist artists who would later form the Ashcan school of painters.

The satirical illustrative tradition has continued in both mainstream popular publications and underground press, zines and comics throughout the twentieth and in to the twenty-first century with the life-affirming work of illustrators such as Edward Sorel, Seymour Chwast, Milton Glaser, Jules Feiffer, Tomi Ungerer, Robert Crumb, Peter Arno, Ralph Steadman, Gerald Scarfe, Sue Coe, Steve Bell, Hanoch Piven and Martin Rowson.

Cover from a picture book of
'Deutschland, Deutschland ueber
alles', by Kurt Tucholsky
(colour litho)
by John Heartfield

German political artist John Heartfield
anglicised his name from Helmut Hertzfield in
response to anti-British propaganda. He founded
satirical magazine Die Pleite with George Grosz
and invented photomontages that attacked the
Weimar Republic and Nazi Germany.

The Eclipse of the Sun, 1926
(oil on canvas)
by George Grosz

Disillusioned by the Great War and fuelled by
social outrage, George Grosz commentated on
society with biting satire and savage wit. Staunchly
anti-Nazi, Grosz's drawings and paintings
documented the 'low' life of 1920s Berlin.

The satirical cartoon

In focus: Peter Kennard

Creative Camera has described Peter Kennard
as Britain's foremost agit-prop artist. Kennard is
an important figure in British contemporary art
and illustration; since the 1970s he has addressed
political themes such as armaments, the politics
of oil, and poverty in his work. He works across
and beyond categories such as illustration, sculpture
and mixed media, responding to urgent current
events with disturbing visceral and haunting
visual statements.

In the 1980s he produced powerful photomontage
images that portrayed missiles being broken by
peace signs to support the Campaign for Nuclear
Disarmament. His purpose was to use easily
accessible iconic images, but to render them
unacceptable. Driven to reveal invisible connections
and communicate with visual impact in his work,
Kennard stopped making montages in the early
1990s and further explored various mixed media
approaches and a wide range of contexts for his
art. He has created gallery installations of broken
and degraded placards and, following the agit-prop
tradition of the constructivists, taken his work to
the streets (via his 'News Truck', which exhibited
images to city workers outside the Stock Exchange
in the City of London). His experimentation with
physical mark-making has included utilising
charcoal, paint, photocopies, newsprint dust and
scanned digital images.

Since 2003 he has collaborated with digital artist
Cat Picton Phillipps to produce videos and digital
montages protesting against the conflict in Iraq and
recent techniques have included painting directly on
to digital images printed on canvas.

Photo-op
by Kennard Phillipps

The satirical cartoon

Our Financial Times
by Peter Kennard

*Soldier
by Kennard Phillips*

*Business as usual
by Kennard Phillips*

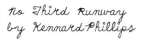

*No Third Runway
by Kennard Phillips*

The satirical cartoon

BLAIRAQ works
by Kennard Phillips

These two works show George Bush (right)
and Tony Blair (left). The Bush portrait is
printed on sheets of the Houston Chronicle that
have been torn to reveal current images of
Iraq and Iraqis printed on Arab newspapers.

Visual codes

Throughout history, illustrations have been used to interpret ideas and messages via visual codes such as allegory, symbolism, personification, metaphor, parody and caricature. Illustration has a long association with allusive messages and visual puns, many of which now form an integral theme in contemporary, conceptual, editorial and narrative illustration.

Allegorical tales

During the upheaval of the Peasants War of 1524–26 and the long religious wars that followed, illustrators commonly used the visual codes of allegory, allusive caricature and satire to question and denounce clerics and rulers. Allegorical images described narratives beyond their literal interpretations and this use of extended metaphor by illustrators could avoid censorship.

Stories were given underlying symbolic meaning, and characters became personifications of ideas. Descriptions of a person or object were also often placed under a different image. Allegorical tales from Aesop's *Fables* to Bunyon's *The Pilgrim's Progress*, Dante Alighieri's *The Divine Comedy* to Orwell's *Animal Farm* and Golding's *Lord of the Flies* have inspired generations of illustrators to attempt to create images that interpret, accompany, complement and amplify the narrative with varying levels of success.

The Hanging (plate 11 from Les misères et les malheurs de la Guerre 'The miseries and misfortunes of War') by Jacques Callot (1592–1635)

The compassionate visual chronicler Jacques Callot is often cited as a significant figure in the evolution of illustration. Callot recorded scenes of daily life ranging from the hunger experienced by many to the luxury of the court and the brutality of war and the suffering of the poor in his print series, Les misères et les malheurs de la Guerre.

Projects ▶

Scenes of daily life

Following the Reformation in the sixteenth century, political awareness in Europe grew with the production of illustrated pamphlets, broadsides and leaflets that condemned corruption and injustice in the church and in feudal society. As war, severe winters, plague and starvation swept through Europe, mortality and death became a central theme of graphic journalism.

Between the sixteenth and eighteen centuries, peddlers and hawkers in Europe sold popular prints featuring the horrors of war and scenes of assassinations, torture, executions, religious persecutions and atrocities. In response to this, rival religious and political groups produced images that were intended to influence the population and instil fear about what the consequences of opposition, treason and revolution might be.

As printing technology developed, woodcuts were gradually superseded by the introduction (in 1452) of intaglio printing and the skilful incising of metal plates and etching. Books containing emblematic pictures, explanatory texts, moral lessons and visual puns became popular in Europe and first appeared in England in 1586, appealing to the Elizabethan and Jacobean passion for wit and allegory.

'The sleep of reason produces monsters'

Francisco de Goya (1746–1828)

Ifrael ex. Cum Priuil. Reg.

A la fin ces Voleurs infames et perdus ,   Monstrent bien que le crime (horrible et noire engeance)   Et que cest le Destin des hommes vicieux
Comme fruits malheureux a cet arbre pendus   Est luy mesme instrument de honte et de vengeance,   Desprouuer tost ou tard la iustice des Cieux .   11

Research

There are many theories and models of analysis that can help you further explore the historical development of illustration and its relationship to your own contemporary practice.

These theories and models range from (but are not limited to) semiotics, communication, media, film, post-colonialism, hermeneutics and Marxism to psychoanalysis, feminism, deconstruction and post-structuralism.

Many of these theories and discourses overlap, which creates a web of associations that can be used to raise questions, investigate sources and materials, find underlying contexts and support your own personal agenda as visual communicator and artist.

Reading as much as possible on the history of art and design and investigating theories that analyse and critique all forms of cultural production will help inform your practice. Apply focused and in-depth contextual analysis to your own interests or a subject matter that you have a passion for.

Decoding meaning

Remember that no illustration is value-free; it will have been created for a specific purpose. All illustrations are signs and as such it's possible to systematically unpick the signifiers and analyse the associations, interpretations and meanings that go with them. For example, take any image that has been taken out of its original context and reproduced in this book and read or analyse its levels of meaning, its denotation and connotation.

Ask yourself:
- What were the materials and production methods used to construct the image?
- Who commissioned the particular illustration and for what purpose?
- What was the illustrator's point of view?
- Which other artists or illustrators influenced the illustrator?
- Is this example typical of the artist's output?
- How are the elements and principles of art and design (eg colour, scale, contrast, line, texture, rhythm, perspective) employed?
- What does it say about the time it was made?
- Where was it reproduced?
- Is its purpose to entertain, persuade, decorate, educate, inform, elucidate or amplify a text, or a combination of all these?
- Who benefits from the illustration's existence?
- How is the illustration seen in different time periods or geographical locations?
- Does it belong to a specific social, historical and cultural context?
- To what category or genre of illustration does it belong?
- What narrative structures are evident?

Panic
by Eduardo Recife

This T-shirt design is a digital collage packed full of psycho-symbolic iconography, from scorpions and bees to teeth, flowers and beetles.

Projects

Project 1:
Photomontage

Photomontage is a technique of creating a new composite image by superimposing, combining or merging photographic images from different sources.

Juxtapose a range of images to reveal connections and associations that relate to wider concerns and issues.

For research and inspiration, look up Dada, Surrealist and Constructivist artists such as George Grosz, John Heartfield, Kurt Schwitters, Hannah Hoch, Raoul Hausmann, Salvador Dali, Alexander Rodchenko and El Lissitzky.

Project 2:
Dada lives!

Tristan Tzara founded the international art movement Dada in Zurich in 1916. It employed nihilism, ridicule and anti-art to negate traditions, social conventions and moral values of capitalism that had led the world into war. Activities included the Cabaret Voltaire, the publication of manifestos and journals, poetry and performance.

Design a series of theatre sets and a poster for a new West End musical called *Dada Lives!*

For research and inspiration, look up Kurt Schwitter's use of collage, Marcel Duchamp's Ready Mades, Berlin Dada and satirical photomontage, *Die Pleite*.

Project 3:
Hey ho let's go!

A descendent of Dada, the anarchic, music, art, street fashion and political subculture punk rock emerged at a time of social and political unrest in 1970s London and New York.

Design music packaging and a viral marketing campaign for a compilation of reissued punk 45s from the late 1970s.

For research and inspiration, look up Russell Mills, Barney Bubbles, Jamie Reid, Linder Sterling, Malcolm Garrett, Bazooka, Gary Panter and Art Chantry, Malcolm McLaren, the Lettristes, Situationists and the Underground Press.

Project 4:

The art of war

Create a narrative or blog that displays the way in which war has been portrayed visually throughout history. Investigate the work of artists and illustrators who have reported on the First and Second World Wars in particular.

For research and inspiration, look up Wyndham Lewis, CRW Nevison, Paul Nash, Eric Ravilious, John Piper, Graham Sutherland, Henry Moore, Stanley Spencer, Edward Bawden, Edward Ardizzone and Linda Kitson.

Project 5:

City almanac

Nineteenth-century caricaturist and social reformer George Cruikshank (1792–1878) has often been described as Britain's greatest book illustrator. Working in the medium of wood and steel engraving, Cruikshank chronicled the high and low life of London (the traffic congestion, gin palaces, squalor, dandies, pickpockets, cabbies, prostitutes, dukes and duchesses) in his own Comic Almanac (1835–1853).

Chronicle the contemporary high and low life of a major city by creating your own almanac.

For research and inspiration, look up the satirical works of Thomas Rowlandson, James Gillray and Honoré Daumier. The reportage drawings of Phil May, George Grosz, Otto Dix, Frans Masereel, Kathe Kollwitz, Paul Hogarth and Robert Weaver. The cartoons of Robert Crumb and Saul Steinberg. The illustrations of Ralph Steadman, Sue Coe, Marshall Arisman and Ronald Searle.

Project 6:

Cartoons for the cause

Walter Crane (1845–1915), an acclaimed member of the Arts and Crafts movement, illustrated and designed children's books, toy books, political cartoons, ceramic tiles, stained glass, vases, mosaics, textile designs and wallpaper. Crane established the Art Workers Guild, creating cartoons for the cause for socialist journals such as the Clarion and Justice.

Create a series of your own cartoons for a cause.

Research political satirists such as Steve Bell, Martin Rowson and Fluck and Law. The graphic art of Cuba, the Ashcan School, Goya's Disasters of War, the poster art of the Constructivists, Barbara Kruger, the posters of Amnesty International and Adbusters magazine.

Imagination is the fundamental faculty in illustration. Concepts and images can be formed in the mind and whole worlds evoked from the illustrator's pen. Through fanciful speculation, imaginary worlds can be visualised and brought to life in tales of fantasy and science fiction, and in legends, bestiaries, myths and fairy tales. Consider for example, L Frank Baum's Oz, CS Lewis's Narnia, JM Barrie's Neverland, Lewis Carroll's Wonderland, JRR Tolkien's Middle Earth or Terry Pratchett's Discworld.

Illustrators frequently collaborate with writers to amplify and visually communicate these imaginary worlds by creating a dialogue between the pictures and the text. Many illustrators, however, also generate their own narratives or interpret and extend fictional alternative realities in a range of formats and contexts.

The examples featured in this chapter are produced using a variety of different media and demonstrate the breadth and diversity of contemporary narrative illustration. The work of illustrators in this chapter challenges boundaries, takes risks, manipulates media and combines lucid communication with interpretive skills.

This chapter will:

Explore the interpretation of folklore, legends and myths.

Introduce the imaginative power of science fiction and virtual worlds.

Review the work of a number of leading international narrative illustrators.

Provide a number of introductory narrative illustration projects.

Dark Rider by Bill McConkey

Bill McConkey makes use of a broad range of techniques from digital photomontage to a more painterly style (as can be seen in this fantastical example). His projects have included illustrations for the New Scientist and Oxford University Press.

Folklore

William Thomas first coined the term 'folklore' in 1846. At that time it was associated with nineteenth-century Romantic Nationalism and referred to the sharing of legends, tales, fables, customs, rhymes, maxims and proverbs within cultures. For hundreds of years folklore, myths and legends have been adopted by different cultures and shared around the world.

Fairy tales

Writers such as Charles Perrault, the Grimm brothers and Hans Christian Anderson have all made a significant contribution to the fairy-tale genre. Many have found fairy tales, myths, ghost stories, superstitions and legends a rich source of inspiration.

By immersing themselves in plot visualisation and by exploring psychological, mythical and religious themes or the archetypal characters featured in the tales (such as heroes, witches, goblins, giants, trolls, fairies, dragons), illustrators are able to create believable worlds that can engage children's imaginations and entertain them with exciting, beautiful images that work in harmony with the text. Illustrators do this by employing strong ideas, intelligent design, bold use of colour and appealing characterisation.

Exemplars in this field include Dr Henrich Hoffmann, Walter Crane, Randolph Caldecott, Maxfield Parrish, Arthur Rackham, Edmund Dulac, NC Wyeth, Pauline Baynes and Brian Froud.

Wicker Man
by Frances Castle

In 2004, after ten years of working in the games industry for Disney, EA and Namco, Frances Castle decided to go freelance, creating work for a wide variety of briefs.

In focus: Priya Sundram

Priya's illustrations employ a rich combination of mixed media and digital collage. The images shown are inspired by the Panachantra-Indian folk tales, myths and horoscopes. Priya is currently exploring the use of collage with time-based mediums. Since graduating from Camberwell College of Art in 2004, where she studied illustration and photography, Priya has had numerous freelance illustration jobs and private commissions.

The Crows and the Serpent (below), Taurus (left) by Priya Sundram

Taken from Sundram's horoscope series.

The Clever Rabbit and Foolish Lion by Priya Sundram

Taken from Sundram's horoscope series.

In focus: Melanie Williams

Melanie Williams' illustrations are inspired by legends, oral tradition and old stories from the Basque country. She describes the country as quite an isolated little pocket between France and Spain and finds inspiration in the Basque country's many forests, rivers, abandoned houses and a species of pony and pig found only in the region.

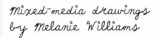

Mixed-media drawings by Melanie Williams

These three drawings were developed for French band Nick and the Mirrors. The work is based on the different facades of every individual's personality and the illustrations arose from imagining the different characters that you might encounter in a person. They also reflect the primarily calm and melodious side of the music that is later counteracted by deeper stranger sounds.

'[My work depicts] a strange and forgotten place where curious forms of life flourish'

Melanie Williams

Science fiction

Often set in the future or in outer space, the science fiction genre speculates on fantastic events and, through imaginative stories, engages with a wide variety of themes. Science fiction writers (and the illustrators who have interpreted their words) imaginatively utilise technological and scientific knowledge and speculate on its influence on society. From Mary Shelley's Gothic *Frankenstein* (1818), to Philip K. Dick's *Do Androids Dream of Electric Sheep?* (1968) and beyond, the field has produced a wealth of sub-genres including time travel, life on other planets, post-apocalyptic stories, imagined technology, aliens, robots and cyborgs.

Precursors of the genre

A fascination for the fantastic, unnerving and absurd is evident in the work of many of the precursors of science fiction illustration, such as Giuseppe Arcimboldo, Hieronymus Bosch, Francisco de Goya, and John Martin. Early landmarks include the illustrations of future armaments in *La Guerre au Vingtieme* by Albert Rodiba and Warwick Goble and Hildibrand's response to the fantasy stories of HG Wells and Jules Verne.

Hugo Gernsback's illustrated periodical *Wonder Stories* (1926) made the first use of the term 'science fiction'. Illustrators such as Frank R Paul, Hubert Rogers, Hannes Bok and Virgin Finlay created a new idiom with sensational cover art and spot illustrations for the hugely popular science fiction pulps of the 1930s, 1940s and 1950s including *Weird Tales*, *Astounding Science Fiction*, *Amazing Stories* and *Tales of Wonder*. Science fiction illustration commonly features on movie posters, comics, graphic novels and computer games.

*Pre-disposal unit
by Dan Seagrave*

This acrylic on hot-press board piece was created for publication as a poster and limited edition art print; it was also exhibited at Fuse gallery in New York.

In focus: Janine Shroff

London-based illustrator Janine Shroff's
meticulous, disturbing and humorous illustrations
and animations of naked 'bird' people are drawn
with biros, crayons, felt-tip pens, inks and acrylic
paints. With singular vision she has created an
unnerving and strange world, exploring themes
such as overpopulation, pregnancy, anatomy,
sexual ambiguity and sexual detachment.
Commenting on her personal work in an oblique
way she says, 'I like drawing nude people and
empty rooms when I am bored for no real reason
[sic] but I can also draw ashtrays and Kerela,
it's hard to say why.'

*Surreal
by Janine Shroff*

In focus: Janine Shroff

Tea Party
by Janine Shroff

Performance
by Janine Shroff

Virtual worlds

Computer-simulated 3D-virtual worlds allow multiple users to interact with one another via avatars (a computer user's representation of himself/herself or alter ego). Artists of the net generation are now inventing virtual scenarios in which the illustrators of the future will communicate, network and conduct business.

In focus: Paul Sermon

Over the past 20 years Paul Sermon has received international acclaim for his pioneering telematic artworks. His practice-based research has centred on the field of contemporary media arts and the creative use of telecommunication technologies.

Through distinctive use of video-conferencing techniques in creative-telepresence applications he has developed a series of telematic art installations. His projects include *Peace Games*, in which Second and First Life converge in a bizarre peace talks charade (reflecting the often absurd face of global politics).

Sermon's work with immersive and expanded telematic environments also includes the *Sylgrut Centre* in the virtual world of Second Life, which combines an artists-in-residence studio and apartment on the waterfront, two flexible gallery spaces and an open plan Skylab research space. This contemporary media arts venue features projects and works for its Second Life audience by artists, writers, performers and architects directly inspired and in response to the global-networked virtual environment and community.

Snapshot of a telematic
environment in virtual
world Second Life
by Paul Sermon

In focus: Charlotte Gould

Illustrator and animator Charlotte Gould has developed a number of web-based interactive environments that explore user identity and the notion of floating narrative. Her projects encourage creative urban play, explore the use of super-real graphic interfaces and search for a new language to represent gender by questioning the predominance of stereotypes and archetypes in many computer games and 3D environments.

Gould's *Lucid Spatial Narrative* project is a temporal and spatial location-based public installation that utilises wireless mobile phone technology and large urban screens within public spaces. The open narrative encourages playfulness and interaction amongst audiences, whose presence is represented as flash-driven avatars monitored via handheld Bluetooth-enabled phones. Passers by with Bluetooth-enabled phones are assigned an avatar that they can customise using images and movies as textures for the avatar's face. They can also download graphics and images and record a one-off drama that is played out in public on the big screen.

Snapshot of characters created for an online interactive world by Charlotte Gould

In focus: Thomas Barwick

Thomas Barwick blurs the boundaries between graphic design, illustration and fine art. Since 1997 he has worked as an illustrator on skateboard graphics, CD packaging, promotional posters and commercial projects for a wide variety of clients from *Building Magazine* and *World Architecture* to *Wallpaper** and *GQ* magazines. Barwick also produces *Ratio,* a fiction magazine and international film review that features hand-drawn fictional stills for film premises that he has also invented.

Barwick's detailed ink drawings also appear in his own illustrated books, which explore the theme of imaginary alternative futures. Rather than following a linear narrative he describes this work as an imaginary travelogue or imaginary reportage. Barwick cites his influences as Albrecht Durer, Constantin Brancusi, Kay Neilson, John Vernon Lord, Meredith Frampton and Mervyn Peake.

*Die Turbulenz
by Tom Barwick*

Unexpected images

The illustrators featured in this section interpret texts using oblique and personal strategies. They make poetic visual statements empathising with narratives in unexpected and idiosyncratic ways. Each one has developed a personal visual language that draws on memory, imagination and direct observations of the world.

In focus: Matthew Richardson

Matthew Richardson has produced illustrations for a broad range of clients including London Sinfonietta, Channel 4 Television, Decca, EMI, Penguin Books and the British Council.

Rather than depicting the world through observational reportage, Richardson's approach is concept-led, playful, experimental and often humorous. Interested in the quirks of physical processes, he embraces the limitations, random mistakes and errors that can be found in image-making techniques.

Richardson works with a broad range of image-making processes including printmaking, digital media, assemblage, photography and collage. He enhances the qualities he finds in these techniques and combines these with his own way of seeing things. Choosing to pictorially depict his subject matter from obtuse angles, his work encourages ambiguity and invites multiple readings. The use of space in his images is important to him both from a metaphorical and physical point of view, and is often used to encourage the viewer to project themselves in to his work.

Patriarch by Matthew Richardson

General
by Matthew Richardson

These illustrations were produced for Penguin
Books to illustrate the fiction of Gabriel Garcia
Marquez. Richardson wanted to echo Marquez's
style of magical realism. To achieve this he
assembled characters and objects in unexpected
combinations and specific colours were introduced
to reflect what Richardson describes as the
'brooding heat', present in Marquez's fiction.

Solitude
by Matthew Richardson

Unexpected images

In focus: Zoë Taylor

A sense of mystery and expectation are evident in the work of Zoë Taylor. While studying at London's Royal College of Art she responded to a brief on the Visual Editor elective, which was intended to push the creative boundaries of the imagination and to encourage students to develop skills in visual storytelling.

Students were provided with a family portrait by Francisco José de Goya to act as a catalyst for their imaginations. The painting encouraged questions about its featured characters and their relationships and circumstances; responses to these questions could then be mixed with personal interests or obsessions. Various scenarios were developed into a visual narrative and students were asked to consider what to show and what not to show and how. The selection, editing and omission of visual information is an important aspect of illustration and Taylor finds it an exciting process: 'I realised that by showing certain things in a certain order I could suggest other things happening that are not shown at all.'

Taylor's illustrations successfully build tension and atmosphere, drawing the reader into the narrative and playing with the idea that what you are seeing might not be quite what it seems, raising questions and a sense of mystery.

Blue Hotel
by Zoë Taylor

The illustrations here are from Blue Hotel, a graphic story about a tired driver that was inspired by a hairdressing scene and a mysterious bandaged man in Goya's painting. The illustrations also allude to the loaded tensions and expectations in films such as David Lynch's Lost Highway, Alfred Hitchcock's Psycho and Stanley Kubrick's The Shining.

Blue Hotel
by Zoë Taylor

Unexpected images

Emily Mitchell's mixed media work combines playfulness, improvisation, observed drawing, printmaking and the nuances of language, balancing elements of chance and control. Through the staging of narrative relationships between people, animals and objects she explores details of human folly, petty cruelty, ambiguity and humour.

Mitchell's work is held in collections in the UK and USA and she exhibits book works at the London Artists Book Fair and the Hay-on-Wye Literature Festival. In 2008 she produced two series of collaborative works for an exhibition with Matthew Richardson called 'Conduits Schemes and Spheres', which explored narratives and the imbalances of power and meaning. The works were described as stages on which different dialogues, scuffles and games of wit were played out.

Wishbones
by Emily Mitchell

The illustrations from Mitchell's 'Wishbones' series explore the bare bones of visual storytelling using the interplay of overt and covert narratives through a series of subtle changes and shifts of relationships and differences between characters.

Feral Coat
by Emily Mitchell

Feral Coat is taken from a series inspired by
'The Red Fox Fur Coat' by Teolinda Gersao.
This tells the story of a woman whose true
feral nature is released when she buys a fox
fur coat.

Unexpected images

In focus: Mireille Fauchon

Mireille Fauchon's narrative illustration work has appeared in *The Idler* magazine and *World of Interiors* and is concerned with time, place and memory. Fauchon's illustrations address not only the melodramatic, but also the quite seemingly insignificant passing moment. Inspired by personal and local history, her illustrations play on the anxiety to protect the recent past and blur the distinctions between fact and fiction. Fauchon says she emphasises the mysterious, transgressive or fantastic and her work strives to challenge the subjective nature of memory questioning what, how and why we remember.

Square Window (above),
Sinister (right)
by Mireille Fauchon

The images featured are from Fauchon's illustrated book 255 Bedford Hill, which is about the mysterious unsolved murder of young barrister Charles Bravo in South London in 1876.

House
by Mireille Fauchon

Projects

Project 1:
Once upon a time

Select a tale from the following list:

- Hansel and Gretel
- Thumbelina
- Goldilocks and the Three Bears
- Cinderella
- Little Red Riding Hood
- Puss in Boots
- Jack and the Beanstalk
- Rumpelstiltskin
- Snow White and the Seven Dwarfs
- The Frog Prince

Research how illustrators in different countries and in different historical periods have depicted the tale and then collate your research into an annotated sketchbook. Now create six images that visually interpret the tale of your choice. Consider your target audience, employ strong ideas, a bold use of colour, intelligent design and consistent characterisation.

Project 2:
Fabulous beasts

Research a range of creatures and beasts from myths and legends. Consider:

- Cyclops
- Satyr
- Centaurs
- Unicorns
- Kraken
- Mermaids
- Minotaur
- Siren
- Sphinx
- Singa
- Baihu
- Gorgon
- Medusa
- Werewolves
- Griffins
- Giants
- Pegasus

Use a selection of fabulous beasts as your cast of characters for a series of sequential illustrations that display a visual narrative in a contemporary setting (such as a commute to work, a shopping trip, a holiday, a marriage ceremony, a robbery, a job interview, a night out, a dinner party or an art gallery opening).

Project 3:
Graphic fiction

Produce a black-and-white cover and six illustrations or a short animated film to visually explore and convey one of the following novels that features social injustice:

- The Grapes of Wrath
- Les Miserables
- Of Mice and Men
- Oliver Twist

Thoroughly read the story and take notes, complement your visual research by investigating the stark woodcuts and lino engravings of Frans Masereel, Otto Nuckel, Lynd Ward, Laurence Hyde and Giacomo Patri, whose work was full of comment, passion and the striving for social justice.

Orchestrate your series of illustrations by manipulating the eye level and path of the viewer; heighten dramatic tensions and psychological factors; create visual metaphors and recurring symbols, and use scale, lighting and perspective to achieve varying effects.

Project 4:

Bar story

Use the painting 'A Bar at the Folies-Bergére' (1882) by French Impressionist Edouard Manet as a starting point to create your own personal narrative. Develop storylines and scenarios and plan your narrative with 20 thumbnail sketches.

Unpick the signifiers in the painting and let them inform your narrative – the situation depicted by Manet, the relationship between the characters in the painting, the role of the mirror and the painting's underlying themes of seduction, selling, entertainment and leisure. Draw on personal memory and your imagination and compile visual references from a broad range of sources. Now edit your thumbnail images to no more than ten visuals that effectively convey your narrative.

Project 5:

Sci-fi story

Design a cover and a series of six illustrations for one of the following science fiction short stories:

- *The Sentinel* by Arthur C Clarke
- *Johnny Mnemonic* by William Gibson
- *Nightfall* by Isaac Asimov
- *The Nine Million Names of God* by Arthur C Clarke
- *The Man who Sold the Moon* by Robert A Heinlein
- *I Have No Mouth and I Must Scream* by Harlan Ellison
- *The Bicentennial Man* by Isaac Asimov

Edit your images and choose ones that anticipate or capture the essential moments and climaxes of the narrative. Determine the motivations of characters and how they interact. Establish mood, atmosphere, dramatic tensions and a sense of place. Remember to keep your artwork personal, meaningful and appropriate to the spirit of the story.

Project 6:

Global folklore

Design and illustrate an information pack that will act as an educational resource tool for schools to teach children knowledge of world cultures and cultural diversity. The project can be print-based or screen-based but the theme must be folklore and customs from around the world.

Survey folklore looking for differences and commonalities and illustrate these connections by mapping links around the world in your artwork. Research oral traditions, tales, music, arts, architecture, crafts, festivals, carnivals, beliefs, proverbs, sports, games, holidays and theatre.

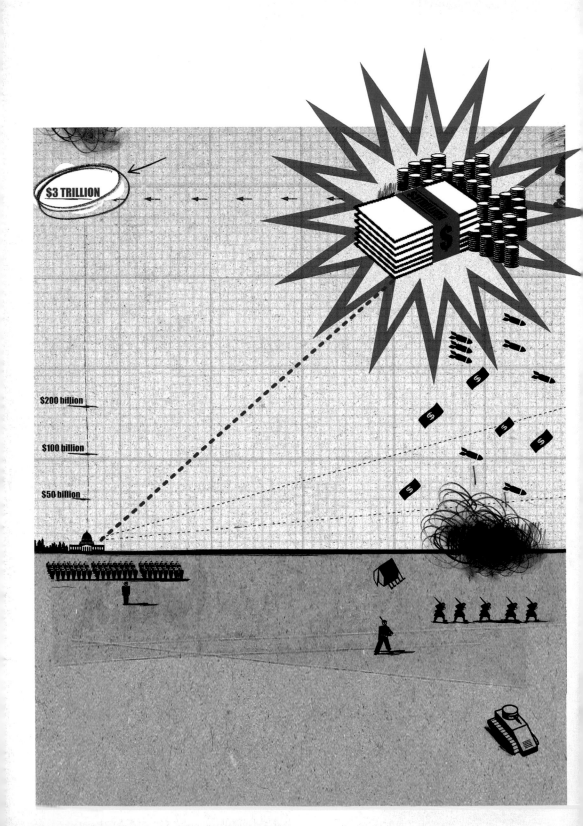

The biggest challenge facing visual communicators in today's global marketplace is creating meaning for people in an international context. In order to produce work that crosses cultural divides, visual communicators must study the differences between cultures and populations. Despite the fact that the Internet has broken down barriers in international business and communication, it remains the case that the world lacks a universal visual language or form of design.

People around the world will have different emotional responses to images based on their cultural tradition and context so it is important to show respect for human diversity and to promote interaction between cultures in the global community. Illustration can communicate in place of written and spoken language and can be used as a tool to promote social justice and respect for different cultures, as well as to entertain and sell products.

This chapter looks at the importance of cultural context in visual communication and introduces the cross-pollination of visual languages from the Far East and the West. This process began when Japanese prints influenced the European Impressionists and developed with western art and design's influence on product design during the growth of Japan's industrialisation in the twentieth century.

This chapter will:

Introduce the use of humour, the interpretation of which varies greatly between different cultures, along with the tactics and skills needed by an illustrator or cartoonist to evoke laughter.

Examine the cultural context of imagery and analyses diagrams and images that are intended to universally instruct, educate, warn and inform.

Provide examples from those who draw on visual languages and cultural experiences from both the Far East and the West communicating to audiences in both regions and to micromarkets across the globe.

Review cross-cultural roadmaps and the many links being forged by illustrators around the world.

Account of War by Caroline Tomlinson

This illustration accompanied an article that highlighted the true cost of the war for the US Government. An Association of Illustrators (AOI) award winner, Caroline's work has appeared in numerous international publications and she exhibits her work worldwide.

Diagrams

Diagrams are usually created for documentation purposes and to explain systems and procedures. They tend to show how something operates and to clarify complex ideas. Professional illustration contexts for creating diagrams include information graphics, wayfinding, mapping, medical, natural science, archaeological, architectural, botanical and technical illustration.

Symbolic drawings

Diagrams are symbolic drawings and they may take the form of a schematic sketch, a plan, a graph or a chart. In all cases their function is to explain and clarify how something works and they often show the relationships between the whole and its related parts. For example, spider diagrams assist idea generation and problem-solving by helping find new relationships between information.

Diagrams are featured in a wide variety of media and contexts including magazines, encyclopaedias, newspapers, websites, signage, blueprints, museum design, recipes, biological studies, interactive educational products, operating instructions and repair manuals. A broad range of imagery falls into the diagram category including chronological charts, relationship charts, graphs, flow diagrams, pie diagrams, bar charts, interface designs, geographical maps and cartograms.

Diagrams are created to elucidate, instruct and explain through a wide range of visual languages and media. If executed successfully they can make complex, specialist and technical information accessible for variety of users. For example, technical illustrator Russell W Parker pioneered meticulous three-dimensional cutaways or ghosted images in the 1930s, he was known as the Cutaway Man for his pencil drawings of telescopes and military hardware. Japanese illustrator Yoshihiro Inomoto also pioneered the technique with his cutaway automotive drawings.

Kraftwerk family tree by Si Scott

This meticulous image was produced with fine-liner pen and Photoshop. The image depicts a techno-music family tree that has been reproduced as a limited edition T-shirt and print.

East/West dialogues ▶

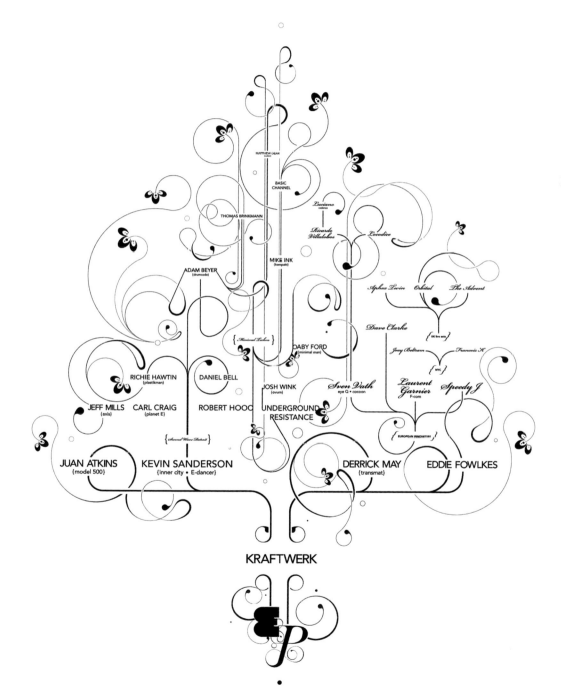

East/West dialogues ▶

In focus: Serge Seidlitz

Serge Seidlitz worked as a designer/illustrator at Cartoon Network before becoming a full-time freelance illustrator. He works for advertising, editorial, publishing, marketing, online content, and television clients including MTV, VH1, Orange, The *Guardian*, Volvic and Honda. His early influences included *MAD* magazine and The Freak Brothers and he used to make his own comics as a child.

Seidlitz's contemporary work demonstrates an ideas-led approach and an interest in a broad range of graphic iconography including character design, maps and information graphics. Combining hand drawings with digital techniques, he has produced a large number of maps covering a wide range of themes.

Many Cultures
by Serge Seidlitz

Diagrams

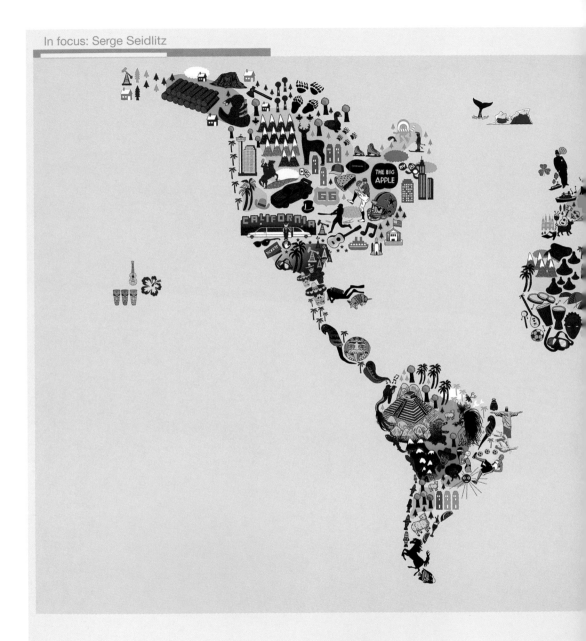

East/West dialogues ▶

World Map by Serge Seidlitz

This image was produced for Vodafone and is an example of one of Seidlitz's detailed and intricate illustrated maps.

East/West dialogues

Within the context of art and design, the dialogue between the East and West has a long-standing history. For example, a sensuous use of line and the flat space, bold composition and vibrant colours of Japanese Ukiyoe prints left a lasting impression on nineteenth-century Western painting, design and illustration. In turn, the commercial art and media of the West influenced the development of graphic art and advertising in industrialised twentieth-century Japan.

The influence of Japan

During the late twentieth and early twenty-first century the motifs, narratives and iconography of Japanese popular culture (such as manga, anime, video games, graphic design, figurines, gadgets, cinema, fashion and music) found a receptive audience among young designers and illustrators in the West.

A postmodern cross-pollination of cultural themes is evident in many illustrators' work and in the numerous niche micromarkets of styles. These styles ranging from cute (or *kawaii*), decorative and naïve to retro, pop, surreal, fantasy, expressive, representational and comic, and all have their own popular followings around the world.

In focus: Tatsuro Kiuchi

Tatsuro Kiuchi was born in Tokyo, Japan in 1966. Originally a graduate in Biology at International Christian University in Tokyo, he changed direction after a postgraduate degree at the Art Center College of Design in Pasadena, California. Kiuchi's initial commissions were for children's book illustrations but he eventually branched out into editorial work, book jacket illustrations and advertising commissions. His first picture book, *The Lotus Seed* (text by Sherry Garland and published by Harcourt Brace & Company), has sold more than 250,000 copies worldwide and he has been commissioned by such clients as Royal Mail and Starbucks.

Golf orphans
by Tatsuro Kiuchi

Sharp decline in stock prices
by Tatsuro Kiuchi

In focus: Hirosuke Amore Ueno

Hirosuke Amore Ueno's work falls in to the hip/retro/chic category. His popular illustrations featuring fashionable bohemians, musicians and funky dancers from the 1920s to 1970s have appeared on Hawaiian shirts for the Dry Bones clothing label, CD covers for Tokyo Rhythm Kings and Love Machine, in a variety of magazines and a range of store displays.

Born in Kyoto, Ueno is based in a Tokyo studio and divides his time between illustrating for international clients, designing retro logotypes, designing websites, playing in a band, djing and lindy-hop dancing. Ueno combines hand-drawn and digital processes in his illustrations and has exhibited his original artwork at numerous galleries in Japan including Rocket, Key West Studio, Art Wads and Space AD 2000. He has attracted a cult, global audience for his stylish imagery.

SEKSU ROBA pleasure vibrations, poster by Hirosuke Amore Ueno

Woman in front of BOAC plane by Hirosuke Amore Ueno

Swing Jack! poster
by Hirosuke Amore Ueno

*Bridge
by Natsko Seki*

In focus: Natsko Seki

Japanese illustrator Natsko Seki moved from Tokyo
to the UK to study illustration and is now based
in London. Inspired by the dynamism of city life,
her imaginary illustrated cityscapes have been
commissioned by editorial clients worldwide.
Her love of historical and vintage reference imagery
lends her illustrations a nostalgic quality, but
combined with witty concepts and an ideas–led
approach, her use of mixed media offers the work a
contemporary feel. Natsko recently held her first solo
show at Tokyo's famous Rocket Illustration Gallery
and is now working on a new children's book.

'Bridges, Sumida River' was a personal work for
Retro Perspective, Seki's first solo exhibition in
Tokyo, April 2008.

'Matuya Ginza' was the first from the series of three
posters for Matsuya Ginza, a department store in
Tokyo. The purpose was to tell its 140-year history
in a pop-up book style.

'Airport' was an editorial piece for American
Express's *Travel and Leisure* magazine.
A collage technique was used to depict
an ideal airport lounge.

Airport (above),
Matsuya Ginza (left)
by Natsko Seki

Cultural roadmaps

Culture provides symbolic structures and meanings through which people codify and communicate their experiences. The signs and symbols that illustrators create are helping define today's global cultural convergence. In this context, roadmaps can offer a set of guidelines that demonstrate how graphic artists have navigated cultural geography and have offered meaning and value to a range of international relationships.

Visible language

Illustrators are magpies and cultural generalists; inspirations and influences are as personal as each illustrator's working processes and style. As you navigate your own creative direction your canon of work will most likely follow a distinctive and personal roadmap that explores many intersecting themes and associations. This personal journey may be informed by urgent issues that surround all of us, such as the threat of environmental catastrophe caused by global warming, the effects of globalisation, or economic and social crises. Similarly, references to emerging technical developments, media convergence or theories and discourses such as semiotics, linguistics, sociology, cognitive science, perceptual studies and psychology can also inform your own roadmap.

Information design

For many illustrators the multidisciplinary field of information design has proved an interesting area from which to express ideas. This area of design prioritises the user or audience and emphasises effective, appropriate and lucid communication over styling. Information design claims to go deeper than most graphic design activity and advocates modernist values and ideas such as designing with new technologies to improve the world and serve people's needs.

In the 1920s and 1930s the utopian modernist ideals of Otto Neurath and his peers were embodied in an international picture language called Isotype (International System of TYpographic Picture Education). This system of pictograms was created to communicate information in a simple, non-verbal way. Neurath's use of pictograms inspired generations of information designers and influenced a wide range of design projects from public signs for roads and airports to instruction manuals, travel information, pharmaceutical packaging, sports events and branding. Neurath's Isotype stick figures also influenced the Otl Aicher's pictograms and information graphics for the 1972 Munich Olympics.

Contemporary teams of information designers and architects use a broad range of production media and design artefacts to motivate and engage effectively with their users. This user-centered field of design can provide you with a broad and constantly growing range of outlets for your illustrations, including:

- software design
- e-commerce and e-learning
- public health information
- document design
- information graphics
- educational books
- labelling
- marketing
- technical writing
- web development
- user experience design
- business processes
- content management

Multidisciplinary information design gives you the opportunity to collaborate with other creatives and utilise culturally specific conventions and knowledge from fields such as semiology, linguistics, ergonomics and cognitive and perceptual psychology. Visual editing is fundamental to all illustration and organising principles are deployed as the content of information is edited and structured.

Every element of an illustration is an individual sign and its meaning comes from its relationship to other signs. Emphasis in information design is placed on creating accessible systems of encoded signs and clear and effective navigation. In a world bombarded by imagery promoting commodities and consumption, information design offers a much needed alternative and critical view on the purpose of design and the role of the visual communicator.

Sahara
by Catherine McIntyre

This personal work displays several shots of palm tree trunks taken in Marrakesh, which are woven around the portrait to create a man dressed for the desert. The palm leaves are also used across his face and in the background to represent the sun.

In focus: Mark Wigan

In the 1980s my work attracted attention from Japanese art editors and I started illustrating for Japanese fashion, music and pop culture magazines. At the time there was an international designers boom in Japan and a hunger for information on the UK's underground and alternative club, music and fashion scenes and the graphic design and illustration associated with them.

Exhibitions and installations followed at Tokyo's Spiral Hall and many galleries situated in department stores. Exhibiting original artwork was combined with designing nightclub promotional material and creating interior design and murals for seminal underground clubs. Illustration commissions included posters for the Suzuka racing circuit, postcards for the Picasso Museum in Hakone, advertisments for the Tokyo subway and murals, new architectural developments and for festivals and the Nagoya city Future Watch Expo.

In the 1980s and early 1990s live painting performances in nightclubs were popular. I painted on stage at End Max, Mix, Gold and Yellow in Tokyo, improvising with brushes and fluorescent paint to a back beat of house, techno and trance music.

Companies were keen to pick up licensing and merchandising arrangements and Japanese TV companies were also quick to pick up on new young artists from the UK; so I transformed my characters into three-dimensional set designs and animated them for TV commercials and programme title sequences for a number of channels.

Boogie Tokyo
by Mark Wigan

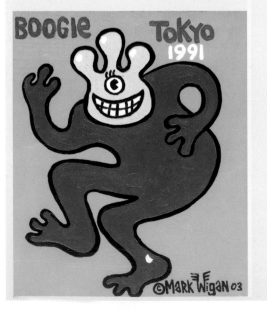

Plankton People
by Mark Wigan

Live painting performance
with Kensuke Miyazaki

In focus: Ayako Takagi

Illustrator and animator Ayako Takagi developed her quirky and cute character 'Uamou From Another Planet' while studying illustration at London's Camberwell College of Arts in 2006. Since graduating, her friendly ghost character has become a worldwide phenomenon in the world of urban vinyl and designer toy culture. Takagi has exhibited at the APN Ink Gallery in Kyoto, Shanghai's Sculpture Space Red Town, at Colette in Paris, the Shihlin Citizen Hall in Taipei and at Tokyoplastic King of the Monsters at the Showroom in New York.

Uamou characters are featured on T-shirts, embedded in plastic capsules on fashionable bags, star in computer games and are worn as jewellery. The latest limited-edition figures are in a series of 30 and feature eyes in the form of black diamonds inset by a specialist jeweller. The Uamou is also cast from glow-in-the-dark resin.

The figures are featured on numerous toy culture websites and blogs and are sold throughout the global network of designer toy shops and galleries including Release the Freaks in Berlin, Domystore in Houston, Texas, Rotofugi in Chicago, Colette in Paris, and Playlounge, Magma and Gosh in London.

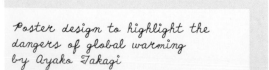

Poster design to highlight the dangers of global warming by Ayako Takagi

Uamou characters
by Ayako Takagi

In focus: Olivier Kugler

Olivier Kugler was inspired to become an illustrator by his artist father and the comic books he read as a child. His influences include Jean Giraud, Otto Dix, George Grosz and David Hockney. Following a degree in graphic design in Germany, Olivier studied on the MFA Illustration as Visual Essay course at the School of Visual Arts in New York City. His distinctive travel and reportage illustrations have been commissioned by editorial, publishing and design clients worldwide and his editorial work has led to a gold award from the Association of Illustrators Images Annual.

Reportage assignments in Normandy, France by Olivier Kugler

Make 'em laugh ▶

*Shetlands to Cuba
by Olivier Kugler*

Make 'em laugh

Humorous illustrations and cartoons have made a significant contribution to the world's artistic heritage, with a canvas that encompasses advertising billboards, comics, newspapers, children's books, caricatures, motion pictures and political cartoons as well as web cartoons and animations.

Cartoons

Illustrators and cartoonists have often employed their skills to look at life from a different point of view and to make the world laugh with thought-provoking and memorable images. Throughout history their images have had the ability to evoke happiness and laughter in order to entertain, inform, comment and ridicule.

Cartoonists create casts of characters and stage scenarios in to which they introduce narrative ideas, timing, motion, drama, mood and atmosphere. They have cultural awareness, intellectual curiosity and points of view, and are often driven to express their opinions and comment on humanity.

To draw cartoons well you'll need a keen eye for detail, body language and human interaction, as well as the ability to capture and exaggerate gestures and lead the viewer's eyes through the cartoon. Just as important as what goes into creating cartoons is what is left out. Unnecessary visual clutter should be edited out and the best images are those that are constructed and selected to communicate and emphasise the aim of the message.

Visual techniques employed to trigger comic imagination include:

- free association
- playful repetition
- cultural references and the use of stereotypes
- contradiction
- irony
- parody
- incongruity
- visual metaphors
- conundrums
- type play
- anecdotes
- epigrams
- comic nonsense
- absurdity
- surrealism
- the irrational
- transformation
- contradiction
- disguise
- appropriation
- metamorphosis
- whimsy
- caricature
- sarcasm
- hyperbole or exaggeration
- understatement
- surprise
- puns
- clichés
- substitution
- transposition

*Chariots of Ire (above)
and Fishers of Men (left)
by Ian Pollack*

*All the drawings in the ink and collage
Chariots of Ire series have evolved from
wheels; hence the title. Fishers of Men is one
of 55 illustrations created for 'Pollock's New
Testament'; an exhibition held in 2004 at the
European Illustration Collection, Hull Gallery.*

King Kong having a picnic
by A. Richard Allen

A. Richard Allen's witty illustrations have been commissioned by numerous design consultancies, magazines, newspapers and advertising agencies. He has won a gold award for his editorial illustrations from the Association of Illustrators.

A Bad Day All Round (above)
and Trojan Cat (right)
by Mick Marston

Bold and quirky personal work produced for 'The Futile Vignette Company' exhibition, which was held in New York.

Swingers (above), Oil (below)
and Policeman (left)
by Paul Blow

Paul Blow illustrates for U.K. and U.S clients
including The Independent, Time magazine, The
Financial Times, The Guardian, Royal Mail and
Popular Science. He also exhibits his paintings
and prints in London, New York and Dorset
and lectures at The Arts Institute, Bournemouth.

Make 'em laugh

In focus: Louise Weir

Louise Weir's work is a fusion of many different working methods and media. Initially sketches are produced and then photographic reference is sourced or recorded, which is collaged together in Photoshop and used as a reference for the final painting. As well as portrait work, Weir particularly likes combining the real and unreal to produce paintings that seek to surprise and disorientate the viewer.

Weir comments that: 'So much illustration can feel disposable and I want my work to be the opposite of that. I have huge photographic library from the last 15 years that proves invaluable when responding to live briefs and inspiring personal work'.

Produced in response to the brief of Celebrity, 'Uncle with hat' is a painting of Weir's Uncle Arthur who was a celebrity in her own family.

'Are animals too cocky?' was created to accompany an article documenting animals' bad behaviour. This shows a monkey in India where theft by monkeys is rife and people are helpless to defend or protect themselves as they are sacred animals.

Uncle with hat (above) and Are animals too cocky? (left) by Louise Weir

In focus: Peter Butler

Peter Butler has pictorially documented the *demi monde* of the city of Hull in the north-east of England with narrative humour for many years. This image is based on adventures in the city's massage parlours. His work is influenced by the social satirist Honoré Daumier's depiction of city dwellers and the nineteenth-century brothel drawings of Degas. Peter Butler works with the cheapest materials: sheets of newsprint, blackboard chalks and a stick of graphite.

Stern measures by Peter Butler

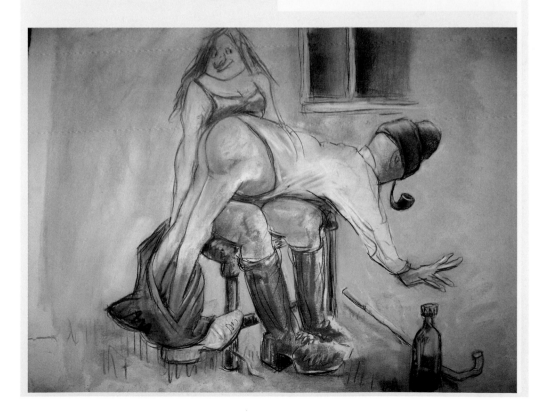

Projects

Project 1:
Information design

Create a visually exciting pictorial bar chart or a graph based on the facts and figures of carbon use around the world or the effects of global warming.

This should be an ideas-driven project so try to avoid a formulaic approach. Consider cross-platform delivery and end-user participation.

Research the life and works of William Playfair (who invented the bar chart) and Dr Otto Neurath's Isotypes (a symbolic way of representing quantitative information through easily interpretable icons).

Project 2:
Cut-away

Create a cutaway or ghosted illustration that shows the details and inner workings of an object that are normally concealed from view. Select one of the following:

- the interior of an erupting volcano
- a cross-section of a pyramid in ancient Egypt
- an anthill
- the internal organs of a blue whale
- a Saturn V rocket
- an operating manual for a twenty-third century illustrator's portfolio and its components
- a city on an alien planet and its transport infrastructure

This project should inform but can also be poetic and intriguing. For research and inspiration explore ghosted images, the work of Russell W Parker and natural science and technical illustration.

Project 3:
Poster series

Illustrate the following quotes with a series of posters:

'Until he extends his circle of compassion to include all living things, Man will not himself find peace'
Albert Schweitzer

'When you cease to make a contribution you begin to die'
Eleanor Roosevelt

'Never do anything against conscience, even if the state demands it'
Albert Einstein

'You must be the change you wish to see in the world'
Mahatma Gandhi

'Better to light a candle, than to curse the darkness'
Chinese proverb

'Do not fear your enemies, the worst they can do is kill you; do not fear friends, at worst they may betray you. Fear those who do not care; they neither kill nor betray, but betrayal and murder exists because of their silent consent'
Bruno Yasensky

'What moves men of genius, or rather what inspires their work, is not new ideas, but their obsession with the idea that what has already been said is still not enough'
Eugene Delacroix

Project 4:
Laugh out loud

Create a series of four humorous cartoon strips, each with six panels. Make use of at least ten of the following words in your 'gag' cartoon:

- frying pan
- banana
- wok
- hammer
- politician
- head of state
- car
- bicycle
- shoes
- hat
- trumpet
- seagull
- chair
- umbrella
- puddle
- vacuum cleaner
- boat
- commuters
- skateboard
- bottle
- wheel
- shampoo
- snoring

Project 5:
Toy story

Design and make a toy using materials of your choice (consider the use of wool, felt, cardboard, wood, Plasticine, resin, paper, clay and string). Specify your target audience and consider health and safety issues.

Now create a story for your toy character. Identify your target audience, consider mood and key dramatic moments and relate your imagery to the text.

For further research and inspiration look at the work of Karel Zeman, Lotte Reiniger, Henry Selick and George Pal.

Project 6:
Postage stamps

Since the introduction of the Penny Black in 1840, the postage stamp has proved a rewarding and challenging area of pictorial design for illustrators. Commissions include popular commemorative stamps, souvenir sheets, sports events, famous people and historical events.

Design a series of postage stamps based on one of the following two quotes:

'Fantasy abandoned by reason, produces impossible monsters, united with it, she is the mother of the arts and the origin or marvels'
Francisco Goya

or

'Our lives begin to end, the day we become silent about the things that matter'
The Reverend
Martin Luther King, Jnr

As illustrators, everything that happens in the world is our potential subject matter and we must be open to a broad and diverse range of opinions and ideas. Your illustration education will be much more than the acquisition of skills and mastering of tools in preparation for professional practice, it will be preparation for a way of life.

Throughout history, illustration has pricked the conscience of society, challenging orthodoxies, raising questions and speaking truth to those in authority. The life-affirming power of the illustrator comes from having a singular vision, self-knowledge and independence of thought.

In 1950, Professor Richard Guyatt described the three interrelated elements of design as the head, heart and hand. The head provided logic, the heart emotional stimulus and the hand the skill that gives form to a design. The world is now facing numerous threats, which are making everybody aware of their global responsibilities. The problems we face provide the heart with the necessary emotional stimulus to take action; we can employ our heads to analyse, imagine, innovate and resolve and use our hands to execute thought-provoking images. By engaging head, heart and hand illustrators can contribute to positive change.

This chapter will:

Introduce the importance of global citizenship and the responsibility that lies with the illustrator.

Explore the way contemporary illustrators around the world are establishing forums to promote the profession and debate current issues.

Review the websites, blogs and magazines from around the world that are used to promote work, post comments and gather information on the subject.

Provide advice on entrepreneurial strategies such as drawing up a compelling business plan and learning to prioritise.

Ideas incubator by Joanna Nelson

One of a series of illustrations inspired by a Roger McGough poem and created for nesta Futurelab, Joanna's bold images combine powerful compositions with muted colours and strong and intelligent ideas.

Head

'Head, heart and hand' can relate to the creative design process. In this way, the head is symbolic of cognitive and intellectual ability, logic, creativity and intellectual and perception skills. It is the realm of idea generation and visual research, allowing the illustrator to generate concepts, respond to briefs and understand the needs of specific audiences.

Idea generation

Ideas are generated to creatively solve visual communication problems presented by a client's brief. Imagination is the ability to conceive new ideas, concepts and images. This creative and resourceful faculty enables visualisation and facilitates problem-solving. Imagination is fuelled by convergent and divergent thinking; the analytical and logical is underpinned by intuition.

Effective ideas often come from generating lots of ideas and then filtering out the weaker ones. Ideas can be generated by listing words that are analogous to the project's subject matter. These lists of words can then be extended into spider diagrams and mind maps, and accompanied with thumbnail sketches and roughs. Ideas can be expanded by making links and combinations between themes with visual similes, which compare one thing with another thing of a different kind, making the image more emphatic. Serendipity can also be part of the process; it is the effect by which you accidentally discover something interesting while looking for something else. During the incubation of ideas there is no such thing as a bad idea – everything should be thrown into the mix. Gradually these ideas can be refined and resolved.

Illustrators are interpreters: they employ cognitive analysis and processes to translate and explain in order to amplify written language with their own personal visual language. During the 1950s and 1960s the big-idea approach to advertising and design emerged and illustrators provided visual commentaries using conceptual illustration that embodied the dilemmas and concerns which effected social and political upheaval and technological change. Ideas were appropriated from a wide range of sources including surrealism, comics and pop art. The concept was of paramount importance and illustrators and cartoonists incorporated metaphors, wit, puns, parody and symbolism with both abstract and representational imagery.

'The place to improve the worl

Research

Research is the systematic investigation into sources and materials. It is carried out to establish facts and reach new conclusions. Illustrators are often obsessive collectors; always on the hunt for reference imagery and building visual reference archives. It will be crucial for you to sufficiently research your client, the purpose of your brief and the demographics and interests of your (or your client's) specific target audience.

A key tool for visual research is the sketchbook; it can be used for recording and collating imagery, creating juxtapositions and reflecting and evaluating ideas. It is a good idea to have a range of sketchbooks including scrapbooks, pocket-size diaries and drawing books with which to experiment with media and techniques.

Critical thinking allows illustrators to place their work in a context that questions society and culture; this enables them to take responsibility for promoting change and draw attention to social and political concerns and the physical impact of the over-consumption of commodities. Illustration has often been used as a tool with which to comment on the world and illustrators have done this with inventive, powerful, compelling and provocative imagery; they have followed their own voice and their own set of concerns. In 1959 Joan Miró described illustration as 'a popular art that always moves me. There is no cheating or faking about it, it goes straight to the point.'

is first in one's own heart and head and hands'

Robert Pirsig

Head

In focus: BISH

BISH cites his influences as David Hockney, Quentin Blake and William Hogarth. A travelling artist-reporter, BISH's drawings document the frustrations of modern life through a working process described as 'a combination of extreme concentration and attention to detail, experimentation and happy accidents, whilst exploring and expanding my own aesthetic'. Direct observational drawings are produced with pen, ink or pencil, which are sometimes taken onto the computer and collaged in Photoshop. Clients include Arup Construction, Orion Books, Jonathan Cape Books, and Jazeera Airways amongst others.

People playing chess
by BISH

Boxing
by BJSH

Truth
by BJSH

Heart

The heart represents the personal, imaginative, innovative and emotional aspect of illustration. It is here where previous experience combines with honesty, memory and intuition to create an emotive response to the content of a project's subject matter.

Memorabilia of a culture vulture

We are all designers in the sense that we collect and surround ourselves with images that reflect our aspirations and help us define our identities. Our identities as artists and illustrators are formed by our imaginations, observations and investigations of the world as well as our unique points of view, memories and experiences. The following is a personal memoir of how previous experience can inform the direction of an illustrator's practice.

Back in the 1970s, my teenage image-saturated world developed from reading picture books, watching animated films, hoarding comics, bubblegum cards, action transfers, football programmes and record sleeves, pasting magazine and newspaper cuttings into scrapbooks and prolific sketchbook drawing. Books, magazines, comics and toys were produced, edited, indexed, archived, and presented in sequence on shelves and in shoe boxes.

Gradually this design activity generated a do-it-yourself art gallery, a postmodern juxtaposition of culturally memorable and personally significant images (also known as the walls of my bedroom). Posters heightened my critical awareness of the visual world and its contexts, the mass-produced artefacts that I stuck all over my walls were symbols of allegiance; they sparked the imagination, captured ideas and functioned as windows into other worlds.

When the World was Young
(left) and The Best Place for
Truthfulness (above)
by Isabel Bortwick

Isabel Bortwick's work is imaginative, figurative
and colourful. Her pencil drawings evoke a timeless
atmosphere of childhood. These images are taken
from 'Stories of the Wood', which is a collection
of tales that explore themes of mythology and heresy.

Posters: a personal perspective

For more than 200 years the poster format has produced compelling and powerful cultural artefacts of their time. Initially designed to promote products and attract attention, posters persuade and seduce us with their visual rhetoric. They urge us to attend an event or to support a cause and are a vital and popular art form that documents changing cultural aspirations and experiences.

In the early 1970s a poster map of Middle Earth from JRR Tolkien's *The Lord of the Rings* took centre stage on my bedroom wall. Designed by Tolkien, the map had been redrawn and illustrated by Pauline Baynes whose work Tolkien had described as 'more than illustrations [they are] a collateral theme'. I would spend hours looking at this beautifully detailed map accompanied with its depictions of characters from the book. For me, contemplating this image acted as a portal to a fantastic imaginary world.

This map was juxtaposed with the visual impact of the iconic *Jaws* one-sheet poster created by film advertising agency Seiniger Marketing Group and painted by illustrator Roger Kastel. This visually striking poster featured the strapline 'The terrifying motion picture from the terrifying No. 1 Bestseller', and bold red letter forms for the film's title, *Jaws*. Accompanying this text was a picture of a swimmer and the menace of the great white shark about to devour her. This compelling combination of text, image and anticipation produced a classic example of the expressive genre of the movie poster.

Further fragmented cultural messages were provided by fold-out poster magazines such as *Kung Fu Monthly* and *Science Fiction Monthly,* from high-street poster outlets and museums such as The Imperial War Museum in London. Finds from here included a reproduction of a wartime propaganda poster of Winston Churchill with the slogan 'Let us Go Forward Together' and James Montgomery Flagg's classic painting of Uncle Sam proclaiming 'I Want You' for the US Army.

Sport was an essential component for the collage of posters, and trips to the Old Trafford souvenir shop provided group photos of Manchester United football club's squad that were updated each year (along with their fashionable hairstyles, star players, managers and football strips). Another poster that would provide a graphic reference point was an advertisement for a local professional wrestling match. The poster featured smudgy letterpress text and images of two wrestlers (Giant Haystacks and Kung Fu) printed on Day-Glo pink paper. The immediacy of this unsophisticated vernacular poster left an impression on me. It looked like a precursor to the cut-and-paste neo-dada shock tactics of punk graphics that would soon emerge in zines, T-shirts record covers and gig posters.

By the late 1970s posters featuring Drew Struzan's dynamic illustrations for *Star Wars* and publicity images of the Sex Pistols and Blondie would enter the blue tacked, cross-cultural, visual mash-up of styles and genres.

Student accommodation and bedsits provided the gallery space for my posters in the early 1980s. The poster that dominated many student bedrooms at the time (and today) was the red, white and black image of Che Guevara that was designed by artist Jim Fitzpatrick and taken from Alberto Korda's 1960 photograph of Che. Symbolising the anti-Vietnam War protest, it became the most reproduced photograph in history and an icon for the counter culture and rebellion worldwide to this day.

At Manchester Polytechnic in 1978 my interest in posters persisted and I would create assemblages and paintings from thick layers of pasted and collaged gig posters that I would physically rip off the walls of city centre buildings and attach to canvas and board. Later I would design a protest poster for CND employing a parody of the *Jaws* poster that had adorned my bedroom gallery in the 1970s. I adapted the image to represent a hungry trident missile shark eating funds that the government could spend on more worthwhile projects than nuclear weapons. The influence of the poster had come full circle.

The graphic languages of posters have mirrored the styles of art and design movements around the world such as art nouveau, art deco, expressionism, dada, surrealism, constructivism, psychedelia, pop art and digital collage. They have reflected people's social, economic, cultural, environmental and political concerns and for me as a visual communicator and social historian they remain an area of fascination embedded in my own personal visual memory, recalling times, places and events.

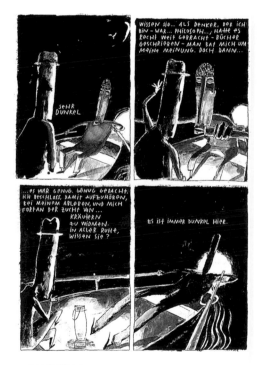

*Illustrations from Salut, Deleuze!
by Martin tom Dieck*

*Martin's tribute to French philosopher Gilles Deleuze
reflects on repetition and difference and uses water
as a visual metaphor for the realm of the dead.*

Guitarre Bizarre for 'Jimmy Draht' #7 by Martin tom Dieck

German artist and illustrator Martin tom Dieck plays with sequential narrative and comic book conventions creating new possibilities for the medium.

Levinas by Martin tom Dieck

A sample from Le visage de l'autre (Seuil, Paris, 2001) Martin's imagery was influenced by German Expressionism and the Dada movement.

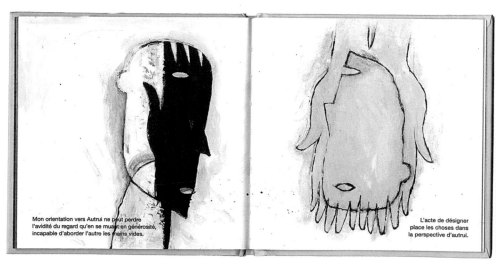

Mon orientation vers Autrui ne peut perdre l'avidité du regard qu'en se muant en générosité, incapable d'aborder l'autre les mains vides.

L'acte de désigner place les choses dans la perspective d'autrui.

Hand

The hand can be defined as making thought visible. This section refers to the execution of images, their production and the interaction between the illustrated artefact and its user. Illustrators use a wide variety of methodologies, techniques and processes ranging from the traditional to the digital and often a combination of both. Every medium has its own unique qualities and challenges and all can be utilised by the hand in any way that is appropriate to the idea generated by the head and the imaginative emotive and personal interpretation of the heart.

Children's illustration

Drawing is the act of applying marks or lines directly across a surface using tools such as a pencil, pen or charcoal. It can be a means to an end or an end in itself. Either way, drawing is the foundation of illustration and all forms of pictorial representation; a visual thinking tool through which you can explore your own relationships with the world. Drawing is also a form of seeing, thinking, responding, discovering, sensing and reflecting; as such, it is both a creative and cognitive activity.

The field of children's book illustration continues to be a rich area to showcase technical and stylistic experimentation in drawing. Artists from around the world have drawn on their own cultural traditions in their work, which adds pictorial comment to an author's words. For example, the work of Randolph Caldecott, Kate Greenaway and Walter Crane along with Arthur Rackham, Edmund Dulac and Beatrix Potter, made use of colour printing and exemplified the nineteenth-century English tradition in the genre.

In Europe, illustrators such as Ludwig Bemelmans created *The Madeleine Stories* and El Lissitzky designed constructivist children's books in the USSR. Landmarks in the field also include Antonio Frasconi's *See and Say* books, which introduced children to Spanish, Italian and French languages. Exemplars from the 1950s and 1960s include Maurice Sendak, Shirley Hughes, Edward Ardizzone, Raymond Briggs, John Lawrence, Brian Wildsmith and Charles Keeping.

Countries such as Spain, Poland, Portugal, France, Germany, Korea, Iran and the Scandinavian countries have strong traditions in children's book illustration and have produced high-quality publications for children of all ages in a broad range of media. Leading contemporary children's book illustrators include J Otto Seibold, Lane Smith, Kveta Pacovska, Gennadi Spirin, Elisabeth Zwerger, Quentin Blake, Sara Fanelli, Isabelle Vandenbeele, Stian Hole, Eva Tatcheva and Oyvind Torseter.

Fish (above) and Stag (right)
by Si Scott

'Fish' and 'Stag' are both part of a poster
packaging series for Resonate/Silent Studios.
Images in this series were created using pen
on paper and Photoshop.

In focus: Rachel Ortas

Rachel Ortas is an illustrator, graphic artist and artist-in-residence at Central Saint Martins College of Art and Design in London. Her silkscreen print illustrations include weird and wonderful characters that look cute but have a slightly menacing edge, which is what makes them appealing to adults as well as children. One of her well-known character sets are the AiAis: monsters from outer space. The AiAis have been exhibited in Magma and in London's Science museum.

Rachel is also one of the creators and founders of *OKIDO*, an educational and fun art and science magazine for children.

Zoe
by Rachel Ortas

Up to no good
by Rachel Ortas

Okido
by Rachel Ortas

Global responsibilities

Illustrators have a big responsibility. By engaging head, heart and hand the can promote tolerance, diversity and social justice, encourage dialogue, cooperation, interpret content and help communicate alternative ways of dealing with these problems through their work and their interaction with others. The Chinese proverb 'a picture is worth a thousand words' is true; a compelling short animation, an inventive children's picture book or a provocative editorial illustration can elucidate and explain a message through visual language faster and more effectively than text can.

Ethical considerations

A seemingly insatiable appetite for product consumption is having a devastating effect on the global landscape. As illustrators, we can effect change, even if those changes are on a relatively small scale, for example, carefully choosing which clients to work with and which products or services to endorse. Similarly, having an opinion about how your artwork is reproduced and the printing materials and inks that may be used will make a difference.

Sustainable development and ethics are now on the agenda of international illustration (as was evident at the Association of Illustrators' Redrawing the Line symposium in 2008). In light of this many designers and illustrators are increasingly aware of their ethical responsibilities and offer their services at reduced rates or for free to charities, community groups and organisations whose values they align with.

Problem-solving

The future of illustration depends on not just following market trends but is instead about innovating, challenging preconceptions, breaking boundaries and injecting some commitment, passion and attitude in to visual communication. Illustration has long been employed as a compelling weapon for social change because it can do more than window dress consumerism; it can provoke, accuse, protest and plead.

Understanding creative processes is fundamental for those illustrators who seek to provide creative solutions to visual communication problems. These problems pass through a sequential process that begins by first identifying the problem and is followed by demonstrating sensitivity to it. It is only then that one can play with uncertainty, generate ideas, incubate those ideas, experiment with various approaches and create unusual and independent solutions that are further redefined and analysed – and this is all before an optimum solution is reached.

*Digital collage
by Aysegul Ozmen*

*Turkish illustrator Aysegul Ozmen works with
layers combining found imagery with use of
Photoshop for CD covers and editorial work.*

As we move in to a new era of global illustration the acute perceptions and individual styles of artist reporters such as LS Lowry, George Grosz, Rockwell Kent, Frans Masereel, Paul Hogarth and Robert Weaver are increasingly relevant. With a social conscience, caustic wit, black Ink and an eloquent economy of line, Grosz recorded the 1920s Berlin of the Weimar Republic and noted that:

'When you take a closer look, people and objects become somewhat shabby, ugly and often meaningless or ambiguous. My critical observation always resembles a question as to meaning, purpose and goal…but there is seldom a satisfying answer. So in place of it I put down graphic marks. Sober with no mystery so people pass each other by…blank spaces remain where they were, I attempt to capture this with the means I am given.'

With so many issues facing humanity illustrators can take inspiration from George Grosz and his graphic marks through our drawings and simultaneously comment on the world, capture ephemeral social scenes and convey our stories to the viewer. Through pictorial commentary you could be critic or conscience and create something unique, beautiful and enchanting. Imaginative, idiosyncratic and ideas-led work will always find an audience; the key is not to give up and to follow your passion. If you believe in your work others in the art and design worlds will also.

In focus: Jake Blanchard

Jake Blanchard's childhood (he grew up in the Peak District) has had a big influence on his work. Inspired by his natural surroundings, his work often explores the human relationship with nature, particularly evolution and extinction. Other influences include ancient cultures and rituals as well as his loves of music and psychedelia, which led to the development of his 'zine and record label project 'Menagerie'. Jake has worked on book covers, skateboards, T-shirts, album sleeves, posters, websites and editorially for a variety of magazines and newspapers.

Animalgamation T-shirt designs by Jake Blanchard

Projects

Project 1:
Greenhouse gasses

Scientists believe human activity has led to climate change, resulting in the loss of Arctic ice, devastating storms, floods and droughts. Create a poster on the theme of cutting emissions of greenhouse gasses.

Use diverse methods and materials to explore your own intellectual and emotional relationship with this issue.

Consider the critical, conceptual and professional issues that might inform your work and for inspiration, research the Kyoto Protocol and the United Nations' millennium development goals and proposals.

Project 2:
Self-promotion

Find a distinctive and personal way of promoting your work in a way that will really set your brand apart. Consider direct mail, sets of postcards, sheets of stickers, T-shirts, gift packs, a DVD sampler, business cards, a website and blog, a portfolio, hand-crafted pieces, fold-out posters, badges and limited-edition screen-printed cards and posters.

Project 3:
Editorial illustration

Create editorial illustrations from five of the following themes and topics to be published in a national newspaper supplement:

- stress at work
- the credit crunch
- conflict in the Middle East
- endangered species
- alternative forms of energy
- 1980s fashion
- rock festivals
- bizarre holidays
- the daily grind

Project 4:

Life is a cabaret

Create six drawings based on each of the following words:

- cobweb
- apple
- mandolin
- hobo
- dog
- gramophone
- Frankenstein's monster
- chinchilla
- balloon
- monolith

Now refine your drawings, select the most successful and consider how these may translate to the stage in a cabaret. Think about how the players might interact with the illustration and conduct the narrative.

For inspiration, research the work of Eva Tatcheva and the films of Jan Lenica, Ladislas Starewicz and Jan Švankmajer

Project 5:

Self

Create an illustration for each of the following words:

- self-satisfied
- self-indulgence
- self-reliant
- self-restraint
- self-sacrifice
- self-pity
- self-opinionated
- self-doubt
- self-employed
- self-esteem
- self-addressed
- self-appointed
- self-catering
- self-absorbed
- self-control

Try to create personal and penetrating interpretations of the words by utilising your direct observations as well as your own memories and imagination.

Project 6:

Aphorisms

Illustrate each of the following aphorisms:

- *'Having nothing, nothing can he lose'*
  William Shakespeare
- *'A fanatic is one who can't change his mind and won't change the subject'*
  Winston Churchill
- *'Appear weak when you are strong, and strong when you are weak'*
  Sun Tzu
- *'I don't know with what weapons World War III will be fought, but World War IV will be fought with sticks and stones'*
  Albert Einstein
- *'A lifetime of happiness! No man alive could bear it; it would be hell on earth'*
  George Bernard Shaw
- *'Be good and you will be lonesome'*
  Mark Twain
- *'Everyone smiles in the same language'*
  Unknown
- *'All these nervous breakdowns are driving me crazy'*
  Lee Hawkins

The term 'global village' was popularised by Marshall McLuhan in the 1960s and was used to describe the effects of electronic mass media. Since then, the Internet has created a global village which, for those who have access to it, provides a rapid exchange of news, imagery and ideas. It fuels commerce, undermines the boundaries of nation states and mirrors global anxiety and concerns (to such an extent that Bill Gates once described the Internet as the 'town square for the global village of tomorrow').

For those with access, the Internet has transformed the creative industries. For illustrators it has opened new markets and meant that it is possible to work from anywhere in the world and to create artwork for clients worldwide. An awareness of cultural diversity and different perspectives on how images are perceived by different groups of people is therefore essential.

The Internet has provided a tool for conducting visual research and self-promotion, exhibiting work, finding clients, sourcing materials or new opportunities, publishing, manufacturing and distributing products, networking with other illustrators and extending discourse on the subject.

This chapter will:

Introduce the importance of being Internet-savvy and how the Internet can help you to market your work.

Explore some of the online and offline galleries around the world exhibiting illustrative art.

Review the rise of the illustration collectives.

Provide an overview and examples from the world of DIY and self-published illustration.

Cover design for *Sharing the World* (written by Luce Irigaray) by Chris Haughton

Chris studied at Dublin's National College of Art. His witty and conceptual illustrations have been commissioned all over the world. Inspired by Asian art, his distinctive images have been reproduced for the fair-trade clothes company People Tree.

World markets

Illustrators today work smarter and reach global audiences and markets by utilising the Internet. Building and developing a content-rich and easy-to-navigate website is an invaluable means of promoting your work and generating feedback.

Creating a web presence

A good first step is to research the websites of your competitors to see what they are doing in terms of marketing and pricing. Art directors and buyers usually commission work by browsing websites so it's crucial to ensure your site is competitive and regularly updated.

It's a good idea to produce separate pages for each service you are offering in order to best showcase your portfolio. Your portfolio should include examples of your work for advertising, editorial, design groups and books and can also include self-initiated projects and sketchbooks. You may also want to include a news page, list the clients you have worked with, biographical information, education history, recent press and your mission statement, vision or unique selling proposition (USP).

Creating a revenue stream via an online store for your goods and merchandise (such as limited-edition prints, artist's books, bespoke artwork, T-shirts, wallpaper, textiles, stickers or badge sets) may be something you wish to consider.

Self-promotion

Once you have your site up and running, you'll need to persuade people to go on it via promotion and advertising. Drafting and utilising a mailing list is a great way to direct traffic to your site because it can be used to send targeted email campaigns (complete with image or animation attachments) to your prospective audience and clients.

Make sure that you include a 'contact me' area on your site that lists your appropriate contact details and any relevant links. Install your website URL at the end of all your email messages and make sure you are search-engine-friendly by hyperlinking keywords that best describe your site. You may also want to request reciprocal links from other sites, submit your details to key directories and check your ranking against competitors.

Employ viral marketing by issuing press releases, joining online forums and message boards or by posting articles and joining the discourse on contemporary illustration while also promoting your site (by incorporating your signature and link at the end of your postings).

'The new electronic interdependenc

Worldwide collaborations ▶

Email Squadron
by Russell Walker

This illustration was created for Ariel newspaper
to accompany an article discussing the use of
Squadron and Fiddler email systems within the
BBC.

You can make use of youtube.com or other similar video sites by featuring your latest live event, exhibition opening or interview. Build a coalition and collaborate with others that share your vision, leverage relationships and tap networks for link popularity. You could use Google and Yahoo clicks, and Twitter.com is a useful tool for getting information and feedback from other illustrators and designers and getting commissions, so you may wish to link a Twitter feed to your site. You could also add your details to illustration and design networks, or to social networks such as Facebook, MySpace or YouTube.

Websites such as ffffound.com allow you to post, bookmark and share images (this site also recommends images to users according to their tastes and interests so it's a very useful marketing tool). Similarly, flickr.com can be used to feature your latest photography, display your portfolio and help build your mailing list. Integrating links to all this activity in your work will also encourage viewers to visit your site and respond to your products.

ecreates the world in the image of a global village'

Marshall McLuhan

In focus: Nishant Choksi

A graduate of Central Saint Martins College of Art and Design, Choksi has worked as an illustrator since 2001. His work has a vintage flavour evoking the atmosphere of imagery of the 1940s, 1950s and 1960s. His humorous characters, with their muted colour palette and flowing lines, are influenced by Warner Brothers cartoons and the cartoonists of the *New Yorker* from the 1950s and 1960s. Choksi has created character designs and illustrations for a broad range of clients around the world in the fields of editorial, publishing and advertising including *Vanity Fair*, Vodafone, the *Guardian*, *New Scientist*, *Reader's Digest*, BBH, JWT and *Wired* magazine.

novelties ad by Nishant Choksi

Fish submarine by Nishant Choksi

GOGGLE EYES

Real "pop eyes"

WHISKEY GUM

It's Delucious!

LIFE-LIKE GIANT WIENER

★ MAGIC ★

NOSE PUTTY
Flesh Colored

POCKET "X-RAY" SPECS

JOY BUZZER
"Shake my hand chump"

ELECTRONIC EAVESDROPPER

"Big Ear"

TRIM WAIST AT ONCE!

GENTLY MASSAGE FAT AWAY!

Just Rub It On!

METAMORPHOSIS

POSITIVELY MONSTROUS

The Surprise Revolver
Looks Like The Real Thing, But It Rings a Bell

DING

HYPN✱TIZE!

3-D HYPNO-COIN

LOADED CIGARS

Louisiana VOODOO Doll

FUNNY PHONY RUBBER POO

REMOVE UNWANTED HAIR
Face · Arms Legs · Body

Life-Size Pin-Up

OH BOY!

POWER OF Concentration
Before   After

Worldwide collaborations

Both students and practising illustrators now have a global platform from which they can promote their work, seek new opportunities, network with others, gain inspiration, find potential clients and join the key debates facing the discipline.

Forums and conferences

The International Illustrative Art Forum was founded in 2006 by Pascal Johanssen and Katja Kleiss and showcases the work of leading international graphic artists and illustrators. This forum celebrates the latest trends in animation, illustration, book and comic art and concept art and provides exhibition spaces, workshops, a film programme, fashion and objects salons, conferences, presentations and a forum for debates and an exchange of ideas between agencies, publishers and illustrators from around the world.

The American Illustration Conference (ICON) was established in 1998 to promote the use of illustration in all media and provide a platform to address issues and develop new approaches to the profession. ICON is a non-profit-making organisation and provides a forum that encourages ongoing dialogue to serve the illustration community, the industry and its clients. Professional illustrators, agents, clients, students and educators and people from other related fields such as design and photography attend and participate in the conferences.

China plays an ever-increasing role in the global cartoon market and the country's Manhua comic books have recently featured at Bande Dessinée d'Angoulême (Europe's largest comic-book fair) and the huge China International Animation, Cartoon and Game Fair (CACG), which is held annually in Shanghai, frequently attracts hundreds of thousands of visitors.

Manga has a huge worldwide following and one of the largest events on the illustrators' calendar is the Tokyo International Anime Fair in Japan, which features a huge inventory of manga and has a cosplay festival and parade with fans dressing up as their favourite characters.

Established in 1970, Comic-Con has grown into America's biggest comic art, film and science fiction-related conference. Aspiring comic-book artists can have their portfolios reviewed at the event, which also features anime, gaming, a film festival, a masquerade, exhibitions and talks by special guests.

The Bologna Book Fair is the world's leading event for children's publishing and has been established for some 45 years. The fair provides book publishers, literary agents, licensing developers and film and TV companies the opportunity to meet with illustrators and discuss every aspect of children's publishing. Illustration students from all over the world hoping to pursue a career in children's book illustration travel to Bologna to be inspired by the latest trends, to network and to show their portfolios to publishers.

Founded in 1973, the UK's Association of Illustrators (AOI) has done much to establish the rights of illustrators, particularly in regard to retaining ownership of artwork and resisting rights abuses. The AOI offers its members business, legal and portfolio advice, publishes *Varoom*, *Images* and other helpful publications, and holds events, seminars, lectures and thematic exhibitions. The AOI is a founding member of the European Illustrators Forum (EIF), which also promotes the profession of illustration.

Speaking at the 2008 AOI conference
Photographed by Russell Cobb (AOI)

The Association of Illustrators' (AOI) 2008 'Re-Drawing the Line' annual conference explored a range of themes including new opportunities for illustrators and ethical debate in illustration.

Worldwide collaborations

Work exhibited at ' Take Away' 2009
by Neasden Control Centre (NCC)

NCC are renowned for creating distinctive,
irreverent and multidisciplinary works. Their
exhibits at the 2009 Take Away exhibition
explored aspects of British culture and food.

Specialist illustration galleries

There are a growing number of galleries that specialise in illustration. These include The National Museum of American Illustration, which was founded in 1998 and primarily shows artwork from 1895 to 1945 (considered by many to be the golden age of illustration). The gallery aims to expose American illustration and to enlighten the world community to the significance and contributions of artist-illustrators such as Norman Rockwell, Maxfield Parrish, Charles Dana Gibson, Howard Pyle, Jessie Willcox Smith, NC Wyeth and JC Leyendecker to American culture.

In the USA some illustrators such as the legendary Norman Rockwell and Eric Carle (creator of *The Very Hungry Caterpiller*) have museums solely dedicated to their canons of work. Carle's museum is of particular note because it specialises in original picture book art. Similarly, London has a number of outstanding illustration and graphic art galleries ranging from the more traditional to the avant-garde.

Established in 2002, The House of Illustration is the brainchild of Quentin Blake, one of the most popular and enduring illustrators in the world. Blake identified a gap in the UK museum sector and with this project aims to put illustration centre stage by exhibiting past and present work from all over the world, giving it the attention it deserves by enthusing, inspiring and educating all who visit.

The House of Illustration offers workshops and a programme of talks for schools, community groups, students and the general public and has curated the excellent 'What are You Like' show at The Dulwich Picture Gallery in London in which illustrators described themselves through self-portraits depicting their favourite things.

Illustrative artwork from the last 200 years is sold in the heart of St James's in London at the Chris Beetles gallery, which is acknowledged by many as housing the greatest stock of illustrators' and cartoonists' work in the world. The gallery's annual catalogues and monthly exhibitions have done a great deal promote and popularise the art of illustration.

Holding exhibits from the eighteenth century to the present day, London's Cartoon Museum contains some of the finest examples of British cartoons, caricature and comic art in the world. The museum's heritage library is home to some 4,000 books and is an excellent place to research the history of the subject.

The Illustration Cupboard is a London gallery established by John Huddy. It specialises in single-artist and themed shows of contemporary book illustration from around the world and sells original artwork, signed books and numbered giclee editions. The gallery works with hospitals, municipal galleries and national festivals such as the Edinburgh International Book Festival.

The Seven Stories centre in Newcastle is one of the UK's leading galleries for children's books. The gallery derives its name from the idea that there are only seven stories in the world, but a thousand different ways of telling them.

Cutting-edge galleries

Many galleries strive to be at the cutting edge of contemporary illustrative work. One such example is Deitch Projects in New York, which was founded in 1996 and exhibited the highly influential 'Street Market' featuring Barry McGee, Steve Powers and Todd James (in 2000). Also in New York, the Cinders Gallery was founded by Kelie Bowman and Sto and was born out of an 'if you're unhappy with what others are doing then do it yourself' attitude. The gallery is more of an art project than a traditional exhibition space and Bowman and Sto often create environments first and then curate people into them. The gallery hosts monthly art shows, live events and performances.

Since 1996, Tokyo's Rocket Gallery has exhibited hundreds of illustrators' work and continues to showcase the best from around the world in what it describes as 'art meets the atmosphere of the new era'.

The street art genre continues to grow in popularity (as the mushrooming value of Banksy's work and a range of high profile exhibitions serve to demonstrate). Urban Uprising in Sydney exhibits national and international street art. This gallery has shown work from leaders in the field such as Banksy, Insect, Faile, James Cauty, Shepard Fairey and Blak le Rat.

Berlin's Johanssen Gallery exhibits illustration, graphics, sculpture and book arts, blurring the lines between art and design. It was established by Pascal Johanssen who is also the founder and curator of 'Illustrative', an international showcase of contemporary illustration.

Ink-d Gallery in Brighton, England sells hand picked work by contemporary urban and graffiti artists. During their shows, the gallery also produces limited-edition silkscreen prints on its studio presses by exhibiting artists. Exhibitors have included Peter Blake, Peter Kennard, James Cauty, Pure Evil, Graham Carter, Brokencrow and Alex Binnie.

Established in 2004, the Soma Gallery in Bristol, England sells contemporary art, design, illustration and craft by leading British image-makers such as Andy Smith, James Joyce, Paul Willoughby, Anthony Burrill, Jody Barton, Austin, Tatty Divine, Lucy Vigrass and David Foldvari.

London's Concrete Hermit encourages UK and international artists to experiment with the structure and installation of their shows. The gallery produces T-shirts, badge sets and books by contemporary illustrators including Jon Burgerman, Andrew Rae, Ian Stevenson, Supermundane and Motomichi Nakamura.

Petro
by Motomichi Nakamura

This is both a simple and bizarre character using nakamura's visual signature of black, white and red.

In focus: Dan Brereton

Dan Brereton is a prolific image-maker working with meticulous attention to detail, employing vibrant colours, a range of cultural references and making use of felt-tip pens and found objects. His work was recently exhibited at the Concrete Hermit Gallery in London's East End.

Shown here are four examples of Dan's work. 'Sidra's Theme' is a felt-tip pen and fineliner illustration for the Five Easy Pieces project. 'Young Turks' is a T-shirt design for the Young Turk record label. 'Late of the Pier' is a flyer design for a track release for the band of the same name, and Sunglasses is a CD cover design which was created using felt-tip pens and fineliners.

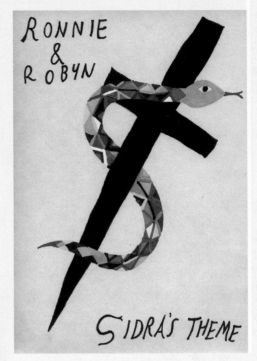

Sidra's theme
by Dan Brereton

Late of the pier
by Dan Brereton

Sunglasses
by Dan Brereton

Collectives

Motivated by common interests and shared values, illustrators around the world are increasingly forming collectives to raise their profiles and achieve their collaborative aims. Collectives such as Peepshow, Rinzen, Scrawl, Elvis Studio, Wooden Hand, Wooster, Spiderspun, Nous Nous and Devil Robots aim to work in harmony and co-ordinate their efforts to realise common goals.

Together everyone achieves more (TEAM)

Collectives with members who have complementary skills will work in a wide range of areas such as art direction, editorial design, installation, group exhibitions, set design, moving image design, identity design, merchandise, consultancy and web design. Members work on both individual and group commissions and project managers are appointed to allocate workloads and resources and manage overheads such as studio rental and marketing budgets.

Teamwork is joint action by a group of people who must subordinate personal interests and aspirations in the interests of the efficiency and unity of the team. To achieve this, goals must be collectively agreed, the workload evenly distributed and communication must be both effective and open.

Working in teams can sometimes be problematic. These may be due to ego clashes, peer pressure, stress, office politics, accountability, commitment to the aims of the team or a host of other reasons. The most effective teams, however, are those where each group member has a skill set that complements the skills of the other group members and where each person knows exactly what their role is (and fulfils it).

Mutual respect, encouragement, appreciation of efforts, listening, sharing, participating, questioning, persuading and helping between group members is important to achieve harmony in the team and realise common goals. Team-building activities can help each of these areas. Team-building activities might include psychological analysis of roles within the team, role-playing games to explore group dynamics and help personal development, group bonding sessions and social activities.

Character designs
by Devil Robots

These To-Fu Oyako characters are designed
by Japanese five-man creative unit the Devil
Robots. Established in 1997, the group has
exhibited in New York and Paris.

Collectives

Project management

To ensure that collective work is carried out as intended, a project will need to be defined and a core team of people should be selected to achieve the objectives. Control needs to be maintained by the project manager and it's also the project manager's responsibility to balance the sometimes conflicting demands of resources, schedules, budgets and brief.

Collective projects are often scheduled as a sequence of steps with associated milestones reporting from initiation and planning through to design and production. Each step can then be monitored through to completion. For continuous incremental improvement, every successful project should be evaluated to see what went right and what can be improved.

DIY publishing

Do-it-yourself publishing has a rich heritage, from the pamphlets and chapbooks of the 1570s to the underground press and comics of the 1960s counterculture, 1970s punk fanzines and today's alternative comics, websites, and high-speed networks.

The DIY ethos is rooted in a critique of mass-produced artefacts and the dominant consumer culture. Its domain is the alternative and the handmade, and the genre encompasses book arts, zines, blogs, limited editions, self-sufficient collectives and online communities. Recent technological advances in digital printing have created print-on-demand opportunities, making the production of books available to an even wider market than ever before.

In focus: Simone Lia

Simone Lia is a London-based illustrator and comic artist. Her cast of comic characters include Chip and Bean, who had a stint in the *Independent on Sunday* newspaper with a comic word quiz; Sausage and Carrots, a three-panel strip created for *The DFC*; and *Fluffy*, the adventures of whom were charted in a graphic novel published by Jonathan Cape. Lia's quirky characters and tragi-comic stories are inspired by overheard conversations, the countryside, a love of unfashionable food, Charles Schultz, Laurel and Hardy, 1980s children's television, squirrels and human relationships.

Shepherd Chip and Shepherd Bean by Simone Lia

In focus: Andy Smith

Andy Smith's quirky illustrations have the vibrancy and tactile feel of silkscreen prints although most are produced digitally. Since graduating from the Royal College of Art, Smith has worked as a freelance illustrator for clients worldwide in the fields of advertising, print, publishing and animation. His work ranges from TV commercials and book jackets to 48- and 96-sheet billboard posters. Combining hand-drawn typography with illustration, his award-winning work projects humour, energy and optimism. He divides his time between commercial and self-initiated projects including exhibitions and the printing of silkscreen books and posters that he sells through his website.

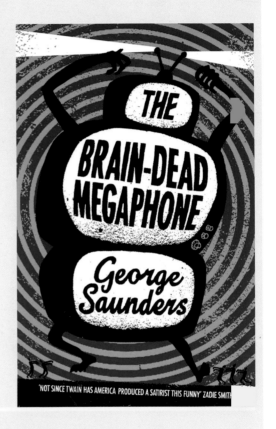

Brain-dead megaphone
by Andy Smith

Brain-dead megaphone is a digitally produced cover design for a collection of short stories by George Saunders.

'I've done quite a few self-published book projects and they often develop into real jobs when they are seen by clients who want something similar. However, when it comes to real work they are always watered down due to outside influences; the designer–art directors are usually happy, but the end client often has his or her own agenda, understandably so, and I think it's important to do work for yourself.'

Andy Smith

In focus: John Bagnall

John Bagnall is a leading figure in British alternative comics. His work was published in *Escape* comic in the 1980s and is now compiled in *Don't Tread on My Rosaries*, a Kingly Books anthology. This group of charming and surreal short stories includes a Berlin diary of David Bowie featuring caricatures of Bowie, Iggy Pop and Brian Eno (shown here).

John Bagnall's black-and-white drawings are witty, offbeat and eccentric. His work perfectly captures the social interactions and mood of the era his illustrations depict.

'Get my Own Groceries' comic strip in Don't Tread on my Rosaries by John Bagnall

Projects

Project 1:
Food and drink packaging

One of the most popular areas for the commissioning of illustration is food and drink packaging.

Illustrate the packaging for the following food and drinks:
- organic porridge oats
- tomato ketchup
- red pepper and chilli pasta sauce
- organic soya milk
- blueberry yoghurt
- organic tofu
- penne pasta
- extra virgin olive oil
- organic miso soup
- red wine
- real ale
- tea bags

Go to the supermarket and look at the products on the shelves. Consider how food and drink packaging makes use of colour, enforces a company's brand message, creates a dialogue with the consumer and harmoniously balances text and image.

Project 2:
Global quotation

Illustrate the following quotes:

'*The world is not dangerous because of those who do harm but because of those who look at it without doing anything*'
Albert Einstein

'*Don't go around saying the world owes you a living; the world owes you nothing; it was here first*'
Mark Twain

'*We are what we think. All that we are arises with our thoughts. With our thoughts, we make the world*'
Buddha

'*In the world there are only two tragedies. One is not getting what one wants, and the other is getting it*'
Oscar Wilde

'*To travel hopefully is a better thing than to arrive*'
Robert Louis Stevenson

'*The only thing we have to fear on the planet is man*'
Carl Gustav Jung

Project 3:
Issues and problems

Illustrate some of the following issues and problems affecting the world:

- resource depletion
- biological diversity
- government collapse
- climate change
- militant religion
- Third-World debt
- unemployment
- urbanisation
- war
- economic imbalance
- population increase
- pollution
- famine

Project 4:
Poetry

Attempt to enhance, interpret and illuminate the following texts by creating a series of images to accompany each poem. You will need to read the text thoroughly and have sympathy for the poem's subject matter and themes. Create appropriate images to convey emotion, mood, rhythm and atmosphere:

- *Phenomenal Woman*
  by Maya Angelou
- *If You Forget Me*
  by Pablo Neruda
- *And The Moon And The Stars And The World*
  by Charles Bukowski
- *Do Not Go Gentle Into That Good Night*
  by Dylan Thomas
- *The Raven*
  by Edgar Allan Poe
- *A Life*
  by Sylvia Plath
- *I Wandered Lonely as a Cloud*
  by William Wordsworth
- *Digging*
  by Seamus Heaney

Project 5:
Marketing campaign

Create a marketing campaign for a contemporary illustrators members club. This should include posters, leaflets, logo, type, design and imagery for mobile media and the Internet

Research members clubs such as the 1820s Artists Society and the London Sketch Club, which was established in 1898. These clubs were social havens for leading graphic artists of their day who were known as black-and-white artists for their use of pen and ink.

Project 6:
A treasury of information

Choose six entries from the following list of themes and produce full-colour illustrations to accompany them. The images must easily be understood by children and must be accurately drawn. Choose from:

- prehistoric animals
- civilisation begins
- the human body
- the machine age
- ships through the ages
- clothes through the ages
- knights and their armour
- medicine
- English literature
- the first Americans
- volcanoes
- man and his dog
- pioneers of flight
- instruments of the orchestra
- electricity and its uses
- the wonders of nature
- important inventions

Wigan's World characters
by Mark Wigan

These are some of the characters that populate the psycho-symbolic Wigan's World.

Glossary

Diagrams

Symbolic drawings such as graphs, plans, flow charts, tables and schematic sketches that graphically display information for clarity and ease of understanding. Diagrams are often used to show how things work and the relationship and interactions between various elements.

Drawing

Drawing is the application of marks and lines across a surface using tools such as pencils, pen and ink, crayons and charcoal. Drawing forms the foundation of all the visual arts. The act of drawing is a creative and cognitive activity, it includes enquiry, observation, speculation, consideration, evaluation and critical reflection.

Editorial illustration

These are images commissioned by newspapers, consumer magazines, subscription titles and trade magazines. Briefs allow illustrators to experiment with new approaches and showcase their work to large audiences.

Fantasy illustration

This genre often explores fictional worlds with references to imaginary creatures, magical heroes, legends, myths, lost worlds, sorcery and the Middle Ages. The works of authors such as Rudyard Kipling, JRR Tolkien, CS Lewis and Robert E Howard have all inspired powerful interpretations by fantasy illustrators.

Idea generation

Idea generation can help produce concepts with which illustrators and designers solve communication problems. Through imagination and intuition ideas can be made tangible with the generation of thumbnail sketches and spider diagrams to create links and juxtapositions.

Mark making

The making and arrangement of marks or traces (such as lines) with a tool. Mark making increases a mastery of materials and tools, extends the visual vocabulary of the illustrator and builds confidence. Experimental mark making and the use of a broad range of media enhances the development of a unique personal visual language.

Personal and professional development

Structured educational processes which are delivered throughout many illustration courses and aim to develop a student's capacity to reflect on and take responsibility for their learning. Personal and professional development prepares the student for professional life beyond graduation.

Pictogram

A pictogram is a visual symbol that communicates an idea, phrase, message or word. Pictograms are elements of written pictogrammatic languages and have been used extensively throughout history to identify organisations and brands, and to instruct and inform.

Political illustration

Compelling images associated with propaganda, protest and graphic reportage. Political comment is exemplified in the prints, posters, cartoons and editorial illustrations of William Hogarth, James Gillray, Thomas Nast, James Montgomery Flagg, Jose Posada, Ludwig Hohlwein, Ben Shahn, Tomi Ungerer and Steve Bell.

Satirical illustration

Satirical illustrations are those that use wit and humour to visually attack and ridicule people, institutions, ideas and behavior with comic pictures. Through caricature, illustrators and cartoonists evoke laughter with exaggeration, analogy and parody to insult their subjects. The tradition is exemplified in the work of James Gillray, Thomas Rowlandson, Francisco Goya, Honoré Daumier, Thomas T Heine, Sir Max Beerbohm and George Grosz.

Science fiction

The science fiction genre is characterised by fantastic and imaginative narratives that often feature projected scientific and technological developments and the influence they have on societies and people. Science fiction has inspired the imaginations of numerous illustrators. Themes and genres explored in science fiction include time travel, space travel, aliens, robots, androids, cyberpunk, imagined technology, life on other planets and alien invasions.

Self publishing

Contemporary illustrators often pursue personal or self-initiated projects with the intention of 'self publishing' their work. The Internet has launched millions of self publishers and web 2.0 Internet generation illustrators sell their limited edition prints, comics, artists books, T-shirts, ceramics, badges and cards through their e-commerce websites and forums.

Three-dimensional illustration

Illustrations with length, width and depth. Work in this field may range from sculptural works and vinyl figurines to mixed media assemblages that are photographed for reproduction in print or screen based media.

Urban vinyl

Casts of collectible characters that are often produced as limited edition series sold in numerous specialist outlets. Designers and illustrators who create highly collectible characters include James Jarvis, Devil Robots, Jamie Hewlett, Pete Fowler and Ayako Takagi.

Virtual worlds

Computer-based simulated environments that are often navigated by multiple users. Three-dimensional virtual worlds allow their users to interact via avatars.

The Art of Illustration

Polyglot Bible 1568

Nuremberg Chronicle 1493

emblem books

Byzantine figure drawing

Caxton's Aesop

Dürer & Holbein

Alciati's Emblemata 1531

Celtic motifs

Lindisfarne Gospels

Bosch & Bruegel

Wood-cuts

Mainz Psalter 1457

Illuminat

Callot

Colour Printing

Hogarths Moral Prints

Bewicks Wood engraving

William Blake

Lear

Cruikshank and Dickens

engravings

mezzot

Songs of Innocence and of Experience

Phiz

Leech

Tenniel

The I Lon

Moxons Tennyson 1857

Punch

chromo-lithograph

Dalziel Brothers

Walter Crane

kelmscott Press

Rossetti Millais

Toy books

Caldecott

Burne-Jones

The global network charts on pages 164–167 are of course subjective, but they do display the possible links between significant exemplars, artefacts and technical innovations that have impacted on the art and craft of illustration.

These diagrams should provide you with just a few beacons to follow on your own personal journey through the rich, diverse and exciting territory. If you wish you can use the content of each bubble to create your own global network chart.

Japanese Colour Prints

Aubrey Beardsley

The Savoy

The Yellow b

Edward Bawden

William Nicholson

kate Greenaway

Beatrix Potter

Edmu Dula

Eric Gill

Private Presses

Golden Cockerel Press

Joseph Low

The A

Fritz Eichenberg

Illus

Ludwig Bemelmans

V. Lebedev

Saturday Evening Post

comix

A

Saul Steinberg

Norman Rockwell

Abram C

New Yorker

Robert Crumb

Alan Aldridge

Ralph Steadman

Quentin Bla

Jack Kirby

Paul Davis

Steve Bell

Sue Coe

Daumier & Lautrec

Lithography

Vollards books

Hokusai

Bonnards lithographs 1900

Grosz

Picassos illustrated books

kokoschka

Matisse Jazz 1947

Chagall

John Nash

Eric Ravilious

of

Wood-engraving

ation

Maxfield Parrish

Doyle

Rockwell Kent

NC Wyeth

Arthur Rackham

Ⴚ François

Pyle

Brandywine School

Dulac

es

Ronald Searle

an Pollack

Paul Hogarth

Gerald Scarfe

Milton Glaser

Brad Holland

internet

ra Fanelli

Apple Macintosh

Wigan 2009

Reference material

Books

AOI
Association of Illustrators Images Annual
AOI (2009)

Biggs, J.
Illustration and Reproduction
Blandford Press (1950)

Blackman, C.
100 Years of Fashion Illustration
Laurence King (2007)

Blake, Q.
Magic Pencil: Children's Book Illustration Today
British Library (2003)

Castman, R.
Juxtapoz Illustration
Ginko Press (2008)

Coe, S. and Metz, H.
How to Commit Suicide in South Africa
RAW One Shot (1983)

Crawford, T.
Business and legal forms for Illustrators
Allworth Press (2004)

Dalby, R.
The Golden Age of Children's Book Illustration
Book Sales (2001)

Fleishman, M.
How to Grow as an Illustrator
Allworth Press (2007)

Foster, J.
New Masters of Poster Design
Rockport (2008)

Glaser, M.
The Design of Dissent: Socially and Politically Driven Graphics
Rockport (2006)

Gombrich, EH.
The Uses of Images
Phaidon (1999)

Gregory, D.
An Illustrated Life: Drawing Inspiration from the Private Sketchbooks of Artists, Illustrators and Designers
How (2008)

Harthan, JP.
The History of the Illustrated Book: The Western Tradition
Thames and Hudson (1981)

Heller, S. and Arisman, M.
The Education of an Illustrator
Allworth Press (2000)

Heller, S. and Arisman, M.
Marketing Illustration, New Venues, New Styles, New Methods
Allworth Press (2009)

Heller, S. and Chwast, S.
Illustration a Visual History
Abrams (2008)

Hill, D.
Fashionable Contrasts 100 caricatures by James Gillray
Hennessey & Ingalls (1966)

Hogarth, P.
The Artist as Reporter
Gordon Fraser (1986)

Kingman, EL.
The Illustrators Notebook
Horn Book Inc. (1978)

Contacts ▶

Klanten, R. and Hellige, H.
Illusive 2: Contemporary Illustration and its Context
Die Gestalten Verlag (2007)

Klemin, D.
The Illustrated Book: its Art and Craft
Clarkson N Potter Inc. (1970)

Larbalester, S.
The Art and Craft of Montage
Mitchell Beazley (1993)

Male, A.
Illustration: A Theoretical and Contextual Perspective
AVA Publishing (2007)

Martin, R. and Thurston, M.
Contemporary Botanical Illustration
Batsford (2008)

Mason, R.
A Digital Dolly? A Subjective Survey of British Illustration in the 1990s
Norwich University College of Art and Design (2000)

McQuiston, L.
Graphic Agitation
Phaidon (1995)

McQuiston, L.
Graphic Agitation 2: Social and Political Graphics in the Digital Age
Phaidon (2004)

Menges, J.
Once Upon a Time: A Treasury of Classic Fairytale Illustration
Dover Publications (2008)

Merlot, M.
The Art of Illustration
Rizzoli International Press (1984)

Poyner, R.
Obey the Giant Life in the Image World
Birkhauser (2001)

Rees, D.
How to be an Illustrator
Laurence King (2008)

Salisbury, M.
Illustrating Children's Books: Creating Pictures for Publication
Barrons Educational series (2004)

Shahn, B.
The Shape of Content
Harvard University Press (1957)

Shulevitz, U.
Writing with Pictures
Watson Guptill (1997)

Stern, S.
The Illustrators Guide to Law and Business
AOI (2008)

Sullivan, EJ.
The Art of Illustration
Chapman and Hall Ltd. (1921)

Walton, R.
The Big Book of Illustration Ideas
Collins Design (2008)

Weinstein, A.
Once Upon a Time: Illustrations from Fairytales, Fables, Primers, Pop ups and other Children's Books
Princeton Architectural Press (2005)

Zeegen, L.
The Fundamentals of Illustration
AVA Publishing (2006)

Zeegen, L.
The Secrets of Digital Illustration
RotoVision (2007)

Reference material

Websites

www.Illustrationmundo.com

www.Illustrationweb.com

www.aiga.org

www.saahub.com

www.Illustrationart.blogspot.com

www.commarts.com

www.noggallery.com

www.somagallery.co.uk

www.illustrationmagazine.com

www.designersblock.org.uk

www.shift.jp.org

www.ycnonline.com

www.theaoi.com

www.grafikmagazine.com

www.chb.com

www.societyillustrators.org

www.bigactive.com

www.centralillustration.com

www.3x3mag.com

www.theispot.com

www.thelittlechimpsociety.com

www.amateurillustrator.com

www.illosaurus.com

www.thesaa.com

www.woostercollective.com

www.stolenspace.com

www.ifyoucould.co.uk

www.kidrobot.com

www.thisisrealart.com

www.scbwi.org

www.gnsi.org

www.dutch-illustration.com

www.gag.org

www.tis-home.com

www.blackbook.com

www.ai-ap.com

www.dandad.org

www.directoryofillustration.com

www.cartoongallery.com

www.ink-d.co.uk

www.illustrationpartnership.org

www.drawn.ca

www.illustrationfriday.com

www.etsy.com

www.urbanuprising.com

www.newimageartgallery.com

www.allegedpress.com

www.houseofillustration.org.uk

www.spd.org

www.bibliodyssey.blogspot.com

www.ted.com

www.itsnicethat.com

Journals and magazines

3x3 The magazine of Contemporary Illustration

Varoom (AOI)

Print, Art on Paper

Illustration Magazine

Illustration

I.D. Magazine

Communication Arts

Computer Arts

Computer Arts Projects

Eye International Review of Graphic Design

Digital Arts Magazine

Artists and Illustrators

Layers Magazine

Dynamic Graphics Magazine

CMYK Magazine

How Design

Step Inside Magazine

Graphic Communications World

Creative Review

Graphic Design Journal

Juxtapoz

Raw Vision

Grafik

Graphis

Novum World of Graphic Design

Arkitip

Before and After

Big Magazine

Beautiful/Decay Magazine

Baseline

Advanced Photoshop

Idn Magazine

Graphic Arts Monthly

Comics Journal

Illustrated Ape

Le Gun

Adbusters

Design Week

Little White Lies

Modart Magazine

Relax Magazine

Swindle

Idea

Exit

Icon

Plan B

Arty

Peel

FEFE Magazine

Annuals

The European Illustration Year Books

Graphis Annuals

The Illustrators Annual (The Society of Illustrators)

American Illustration

Harper Collins International

Images Annual

Association of Illustrators

Writers and Artists Year Book

Children's Writers Year Book

Contact

The Art Book

The Black Book

Le Book

BIG

Luerzers 200 Best Illustrators Worldwide

Illustration File Japan

The I Spot

Creative Review Annual

The Black Book

D & AD Annual

Contacts

A. Richard Allen
www.illoz.com/arichardallen
Page 110

Al Heighton
www.alanheighton.co.uk
me@alanheighton.co.uk
Page 31

Andy Smith
www.asmithillustration.com
andy@asmithillustration.com
Page 156

Ayako Takagi
www.uamou.com
Pages 104–105

Aysegul Ozmen
www.aysegulozmen.com
Page 133

Bill McConkey
info@debutart.com
Page 58

Bish
www.bishbash.me.uk
bish@bishbash.me.uk
Pages 120, 121

Caroline Tomlinson
www.carolinetomlinson.com
info@carolinetomlinson.com
Page 86

Cat Picton Phillips
www.kennardphillipps.com
Pages 47, 48–49, 50–51

Catherine McIntyre
www.members.madasafish.
com/~cmci/
cmcimagine@btinternet.com
Pages 100–101

Charlotte Gould
Page 74

Chris Haughton
www.vegetablefriedrice.com
chris@vegetablefriedrice.com
Pages 138–139

Dan Seagrave
www.danseagrave.com
Page 67

Daniel Brereton
www.danhaspotential.com
Pages 150–151

David Fulford
www.david-fulford.com
david.fulford@network.rca.
ac.uk
Pages 22–23

Devil Robots
www.dvrb.jp/w
Page 153

Eduardo Recife
www.misprintedtype.com
Pages 6, 55

Emily Mitchell
Pages 80–81

Frances Castle
www.smallmoonvalley.com
Pages 16, 15, 26–27, 61

Frazer Hudson
www.frazerhudson.com
Page 28

Gary Embury
www.embury.co.uk
Pages 2–3

Gemma Correll
www.gemmacorrell.com
gemmacorrell@hotmail.com
Pages 12, 24–25

Hirosuke Amore
www.monster-mix.com
amore@love.email.ne.jp
Pages 96–97

Ian Pollock
ian.pollock21@ntlworld.com
Page 109

Isabel Bostwick
bee@isabelbostwick.com
isabelbostwick@yahoo.co.uk
Pages 122, 127

Izzie Klingels
www.izzieklingels.com
Page 9

Jake Blanchford
www.jakeblanchard.co.uk
jaketb@gmail.com
Pages 134–135

Janine Shroff
www.janineshroff.co.uk
Pages 68–69, 70–71

Joanna Nelson
www.giantillustration.com
Jo@giantillustration.com
Page 116

John Bagnall
john@bagpen.fsnet.co.uk
Page 157

Louise Weir
www.louiseweir.com
Page 112

Conclusion/Acknowledgements ▶

Mario Hugo
www.mariohugo.com
Pages 20–21

Mark Wigan
www.wigansworld.moonfruit.
com
markwigan@hotmail.com
Pages 102–103, 164–165,
166–167, 172–173

Martin Tom Dieck
www.mtomdieck.net
Pages 125, 126–127

Matthew Richardson
matthew@hoofandclaw.co.uk
Pages 76–77

Melanie Williams
www.williams-melanie.co.uk
mela_wil@yahoo.co.uk
Pages 64–65

Mick Marston
www.thefutilevignette.com
info@thefutilevignette.com
Page 110

Mike Redmond
mike-redmond@hotmail.com
Page 14

Mireille Fauchon
www.mireillefauchon.com
Pages 82–83

Motomichi Nakamura
www.motomichi.com
Page 149

Natsko Seki
www.natsko.com
helen@agencyrush.com
(for commission only)
Pages 98–99

Neasden Control Centre
www.neasdoncontrolcentre.
com
Page 146

Nishant Choksi
www.nishantchoksi.com
Pages 142–143

Olivier Kugler
www.olivierkugler.com
Pages 106–107

Paul Blow
paul@paulblow.com
Page 111

Paul Bowman
bowman1@dircon.co.uk
Page 40

Paul Sermon
www.paulsermon.org
Page 73

Peter Butler
(care of)
markwigan@hotmail.com
Page 113

Peter Kennard
www.kennardphillipps.com
Pages 47, 48–49, 50–51

Priya Sundram
www.priyasundram.com
priyatheplant@hotmail.com
Pages 62–63

Rachel Ortas
www.rachelortas.co.uk
rachelortas@hotmail.com
Pages 130–131

Russell walker
russell@fetch.orangehome.
co.uk
Page 141

Serge Seidlitz
www.sergeseidlitz.com
Pages 90–91, 92–93

Si Scott
www.siscottstudio.com
Pages 89, 129

Simone Lia
www.simonelia.com
simone@simonelia.com
Pages 154–155

Tatsuro Kiuchi
www.tatsurokiuchi.com
info@tatsurokiuchi.com
Pages 94–95

Thomas Barwick
www.thomasbarwick.com
tom.barwick@virgin.net
Pages 41, 75

Zoe Taylor
zlysbeth@hotmail.com
Pages 78–79

Conclusion

Conclusion

As a visual communicator, I am concerned with the communication of ideas and using the language of contemporary culture and media as a vehicle with no separation or distinction in status between the mediums of art, technology, music, fashion, illustration and design.

From the core of the cultural zeitgeist, fundamental questions are coming to the fore for all visual communicators. Who is it that gains from the images we make? What are the social and environmental costs of their production? Do terms such 'responsibility', 'ethics', 'global citizenship', 'integrity', 'sustainable development' and 'mature values' have any place in the education of the illustrator?

As illustrators, our imaginations and creativity can be used to do more than just decorate commodities; we can tell stories, comment on the world, highlight injustice, solve problems and communicate meaningful content that will benefit humanity.

As I have been writing this book, the burning of fossil fuels continues to cause a scarcity of resources. There is a gradual increase in the earth's surface temperature and changes in weather patterns. The global economy is in a recession and the global political landscape is in a constant state of flux. As such, there's plenty to comment on and who better than the illustrator to do it.

Acknowledgements

I would like to thank the international illustrators who contributed images, words and time to this project.

I am grateful for all I have learned from my colleagues and from my students at Derby and Coventry Universities, Central Saint Martins College of Art and Design, Camberwell College of Arts and The University of Salford. Also thanks to the many artists, art directors, editors, designers, agents and illustrators I have collaborated with.

A special thanks to Kerry Baldry for all the time and effort she has put into helping make this book possible.

Thanks to Darren Lever for the book's cover and page design and a final thank you for the efforts of Caroline Walmsley, Brian Morris, Helen Stone and all at AVA Publishing.

Picture credits

Publisher's note

The subject of ethics is not new, yet its consideration within the applied visual arts is perhaps not as prevalent as it might be. Our aim here is to help a new generation of students, educators and practitioners find a methodology for structuring their thoughts and reflections in this vital area.

AVA Publishing hopes that these **Working with ethics** pages provide a platform for consideration and a flexible method for incorporating ethical concerns in the work of educators, students and professionals. Our approach consists of four parts:

The **introduction** is intended to be an accessible snapshot of the ethical landscape, both in terms of historical development and current dominant themes.

The **framework** positions ethical consideration into four areas and poses questions about the practical implications that might occur. Marking your response to each of these questions on the scale shown will allow your reactions to be further explored by comparison.

The **case study** sets out a real project and then poses some ethical questions for further consideration. This is a focus point for a debate rather than a critical analysis so there are no predetermined right or wrong answers.

A selection of **further reading** for you to consider areas of particular interest in more detail.

Ethical: aware-ness/ reflect-ion/ debate

Working with ethics

Introduction

Ethics is a complex subject that interlaces the idea of responsibilities to society with a wide range of considerations relevant to the character and happiness of the individual. It concerns virtues of compassion, loyalty and strength, but also of confidence, imagination, humour and optimism. As introduced in ancient Greek philosophy, the fundamental ethical question is *what should I do?* How we might pursue a 'good' life not only raises moral concerns about the effects of our actions on others, but also personal concerns about our own integrity.

In modern times the most important and controversial questions in ethics have been the moral ones. With growing populations and improvements in mobility and communications, it is not surprising that considerations about how to structure our lives together on the planet should come to the forefront. For visual artists and communicators it should be no surprise that these considerations will enter into the creative process.

Some ethical considerations are already enshrined in government laws and regulations or in professional codes of conduct. For example, plagiarism and breaches of confidentiality can be punishable offences. Legislation in various nations makes it unlawful to exclude people with disabilities from accessing information or spaces. The trade of ivory as a material has been banned in many countries. In these cases, a clear line has been drawn under what is unacceptable.

But most ethical matters remain open to debate, among experts and lay-people alike, and in the end we have to make our own choices on the basis of our own guiding principles or values. Is it more ethical to work for a charity than for a commercial company? Is it unethical to create something that others find ugly or offensive?

Specific questions such as these may lead to other questions that are more abstract. For example, is it only effects on humans (and what they care about) that are important, or might effects on the natural world require attention too?

Is promoting ethical consequences justified even when it requires ethical sacrifices along the way? Must there be a single unifying theory of ethics (such as the Utilitarian thesis that the right course of action is always the one that leads to the greatest happiness of the greatest number), or might there always be many different ethical values that pull a person in various directions?

As we enter into ethical debate and engage with these dilemmas on a personal and professional level, we may change our views or change our view of others. The real test though is whether, as we reflect on these matters, we change the way we act as well as the way we think. Socrates, the 'father' of philosophy, proposed that people will naturally do 'good' if they know what is right. But this point might only lead us to yet another question: *how do we know what is right?*

You
What are your ethical beliefs?

Central to everything you do will be your attitude to people and issues around you. For some people their ethics are an active part of the decisions they make everyday as a consumer, a voter or a working professional. Others may think about ethics very little and yet this does not automatically make them unethical. Personal beliefs, lifestyle, politics, nationality, religion, gender, class or education can all influence your ethical viewpoint.

Using the scale, where would you place yourself? What do you take into account to make your decision? Compare results with your friends or colleagues.

Your client
What are your terms?

Working relationships are central to whether ethics can be embedded into a project and your conduct on a day-to-day basis is a demonstration of your professional ethics. The decision with the biggest impact is whom you choose to work with in the first place. Cigarette companies or arms traders are often-cited examples when talking about where a line might be drawn, but rarely are real situations so extreme. At what point might you turn down a project on ethical grounds and how much does the reality of having to earn a living effect your ability to choose?

Using the scale, where would you place a project? How does this compare to your personal ethical level?

01 02 03 04 05 06 07 08 09 10

01 02 03 04 05 06 07 08 09 10

Your specifications
What are the impacts of
your materials?

In relatively recent times we are
learning that many natural materials
are in short supply. At the same
time we are increasingly aware that
some man-made materials can have
harmful, long-term effects on people
or the planet. How much do you know
about the materials that you use?
Do you know where they come from,
how far they travel and under what
conditions they are obtained? When
your creation is no longer needed,
will it be easy and safe to recycle?
Will it disappear without a trace? Are
these considerations the responsibility
of you or are they out of your hands?

Using the scale, mark how ethical your
material choices are.

Your creation
What is the purpose of your work?

Between you, your colleagues and
an agreed brief, what will your creation
achieve? What purpose will it have
in society and will it make a positive
contribution? Should your work result
in more than commercial success or
industry awards? Might your creation
help save lives, educate, protect
or inspire? Form and function are
two established aspects of judging
a creation, but there is little consensus
on the obligations of visual artists
and communicators toward society,
or the role they might have in solving
social or environmental problems.
If you want recognition for being the
creator, how responsible are you for
what you create and where might that
responsibility end?

Using the scale, mark how ethical
the purpose of your work is.

01 02 03 04 05 06 07 08 09 10

01 02 03 04 05 06 07 08 09 10

Working with ethics

One aspect of illustration that raises an ethical dilemma is that of creating satirical drawings that can depict people in fictional situations. In satire, issues are ridiculed or derided and although a sketch is usually meant to be funny, the purpose is often to attack something which the illustrator disapproves of. Cruel caricatures and exaggeration can be used both to amuse and to encourage debate. Sometimes, the more ridiculous an illustration becomes, the better it can be at raising a point and making viewers think – political cartoons are one example. But what is funny and thought-provoking to one person can very often be highly offensive and infuriating to another. Is it up to an illustrator to know the difference between intelligent provocation and extreme bad taste, or should viewers accept that satirical illustrations must cause offence in some form if they are to fulfil their role?

In 1953, the US Senate Subcommittee to Investigate Juvenile Delinquency formed to consider the causes of juvenile crime. In 1954, it opened hearings looking specifically at the influences of the comic book industry. In evidence against comic books, various examples of horror comics were used. Storylines of children killing their parents, men playing baseball with a dead man's head and grossly deformed women were all exhibited.

While the sub-committee adjourned to consider their actions, civic groups, retailers and other politicians urged the industry to clean up its own act. In response, all publishers (apart from three) formed the Comics Magazine Association of America (CMAA) and appointed New York City magistrate Charles F Murphy as the 'comics czar'. His job was to create and enforce a code of standards to regain the trust of the general public.

The new standards forbade showing any sympathy towards criminal activity and declared that no disrespect could be shown toward authorities such as the police, government or other 'respected institutions'. It banned the words 'horror' and 'terror' from appearing on covers and strictly disallowed insults or attacks on religious or racial groups. Women were not be drawn in 'salacious' dress. Respect for parents and 'honourable behaviour' should be shown at all times. In these and other outlined ways, the CMAA publicly declared its moral responsibility for American youth.

In 1955, the Senate Subcommittee published its own conclusions and resolved to keep a watchful eye on the CMAA code. In the same year, thirteen States enacted laws either prohibiting sales of crime and horror comic books to minors or banning them outright. By 1956, controversy over comic book content had effectively ended and concerns over juvenile delinquency shifted to television, film and rock and roll.

A revision of the code unexpectedly came about in 1970 after President Nixon's Department of Health, Education and Welfare asked Marvel Comics to incorporate an anti-drug storyline in one of its major titles. In a three-part story, Peter Parker's best friend starts taking drugs and Peter confronts the dealers; Spider-Man saves the man 'stoned right out of his mind' after he walks off a building thinking that he can fly. But the CMAA code did not allow any depiction of drugs and therefore it did not gain immediate CMAA approval. Despite this, Marvel published the story, it proved to be a best-seller, and as a consequence the code was revised to reflect the attitudes of the more liberal reading general public. As a result, some publishers launched new horror content, but none returned to the level of gore previously seen in the 1950s.

Is it unethical to illustrate criminal activity?

Do codes of practice make professions more ethical?

Would you illustrate a Government publication?

I prefer drawing to talking. Drawing is faster, and leaves less room for lies.

Le Corbusier

Working with ethics

Further reading

AIGA
Design business and ethics
2007, AIGA

Eaton, Marcia Muelder
Aesthetics and the good life
1989, Associated University Press

Ellison, David
Ethics and aesthetics in European modernist literature
2001, Cambridge University Press

Fenner, David EW (Ed.)
Ethics and the arts: an anthology
1995, Garland Reference Library of Social Science

Gini, Al (Ed.)
Case studies in business ethics
2005, Prentice Hall

McDonough, William and Braungart, Michael
'Cradle to Cradle: Remaking the Way We Make Things'
2002

Papanek, Victor
'Design for the Real World: Making to Measure'
1971

United Nations
Global Compact the Ten Principles www.unglobalcompact.org/
AboutTheGC/TheTenPrinciples/index.html